OCCULT
EXPLOSION

OCCULT

EXPLOSION

DAVID MARSHALL

An investigation of Justin's story
led into a world of dark forces
that drive behaviour, and the
establishment of a link between
Drugs, Rock-Rave and the Occult.

AUTUMN

HOUSE

Copyright © 1997 by David Marshall

First published in 1997

ISBN 1-873796-68-4

Published by
Autumn House
Alma Park, Grantham, Lincolnshire,
NG31 9SL, England

The Author

David Marshall is an investigative journalist who has authored ten books. He has a first degree, a PhD, and is a book and magazine editor.

A child of the sixties, Dr Marshall started on the fourteen-month investigation that produced this book after the suicide-in-suspicious-circumstances of the 18-year-old son of a family whom he knew very well. The inquiry led him through the drug culture and the Rock-Rave scene to the murky realm of the occult.

THANK YOU

In his research into the world of Rock, Heavy Metal, Kerrang and Rave, the author was assisted by Vivienne James, a Cambridge undergraduate. He wishes to thank Vivienne, and Dr John Walton of St Andrews University, Miss Nan Tucker, Dr Hugh Dunton and Richard J. B. Willis for painstakingly checking the accuracy of the manuscript.

Other books by David Marshall (published by Autumn House) include:

THE DEVIL HIDES OUT: New Age and the Occult,
    a Christian Perspective
NEW AGE VERSUS THE GOSPEL
THE BATTLE FOR THE BOOK
WHERE JESUS WALKED
PILGRIM WAYS
FOOTPRINTS OF PAUL
THE BOUNTY BIBLE

Note. For legal reasons the names of those involved in Justin's story and Cherie's story have been changed.

OCCULT
EXPLOSION

Contents

FOREWORD BY
JENNIFER REES LARCOMBE

This is not a nice book. It will certainly fascinate you, but the subject that it covers is dark, sinister and often distressing. I OUGHT to warn you not to read it if you are squeamish, prone to nightmares and afraid of the dark. But I can't say that, because I believe passionately that you MUST read it — however upsetting you may find it. If you are between 10 and 20, it is vital that you get into it as fast as you can, if you are a parent, a godparent, a grandparent or a fond uncle or aunt, you too should read it as soon as possible. If you run any kind of youth group, church-based or otherwise, or if you are a teacher, this book is also a must.

People will probably say that it is unwise to read books on the occult, and there may be sense in what they say. Like a moth is attracted to a candle flame, books on the occult can seem deeply fascinating, and many people have been sucked into danger by reading too many of them. Yet to ignore the occult or to pretend the events this book describes do not happen, that too is dangerous. We need to face the ugly fact that drugs, Rock-Rave and the occult wield massive power over many lives today. To be forewarned is to be forearmed.

It would be easy to think of this book as just being of interest to young people or for those involved with them, but I think that would be sad. It should be read by far more people than that because it will cause us to pray.

If we do not take spiritual warfare seriously, the horrible things this book describes will continue to engulf our nation. We are NOT powerless against this invasion, we can assist the armies of heaven in their fight against darkness, simply by praying. Do read it, so that you will know what we are up against — and then go into battle!

Jennifer Rees Larcombe is the author of *Unexpected Healing, Stone of Evil* and *Dance to the Music* among many other books (all published by Hodder & Stoughton).

OCCULT
EXPLOSION

QUESTIONS THAT DEMAND ANSWERS

What was it that drove Justin into drugs? How could the Rock-Rave scene, which had absorbed his attention, have so driven his behaviour? The occult symbols, and the menacing 'voices' delivering such detailed instructions: Where had they come from?

'Suicide by drowning' was the Coroner's verdict. But, in the tunnel-of-mystery that was Justin's life, had there been dark forces lurking in the shadows that could have impelled him to his death?

Justin is dead. But his killers are on the loose and claiming more victims by the day. Should they not be identified?

Hard Rock, Heavy Metal, Kerrang and Rave music. Is there any substance in 'the Satanic connection', beyond the PR packaging of the bands? Is there a connection between the lyrics and the behaviour of those who listen to them? Is there anything in the very nature of the sustained thunder, tantric beat and photic lighting of an all-night Rave that could lead to permanent personality changes and driven behaviour?

How does the occult impact on the Hard Rock-Rave scene?

What is the occult? Why has there been an occult explosion in Western society since the mid-sixties? What is the source of the paranormal? Why do New Age, Astrology, Spiritualism and Satanism hold such a fascination for so many?

Cherie got into the drugs-occult-Heavy Metal scene, but wanted out. How can we help those who want out? Are there grounds for believing in a clash of kingdoms in the realm of the supernatural? Is it possible for such a clash to occur over the life of an individual?

Drugs, Rock-Rave and the Occult: Is there a connection?

What can Christians offer as an alternative to a generation besotted by all three? Can we identify the doors through which the Evil Empire gains access to lives — and slam them shut?

Through an investigation of Justin's and Cherie's stories, we have sought to answer all these questions — and to base our answers on hard evidence, and the Rock that doesn't roll.

Tripping into Rave

Whether Justin's troubles began with the death of his mother, or long before, is a matter for conjecture. He was 13 when cancer killed her; and her major preoccupation in the weeks during which she watched death's stealthy approach was, 'How will Justin cope when I'm gone?'

Justin had a lot going for him. He was a well-built boy with a pleasant disposition and a place at a highly selective English grammar school. But 'outgoing' was the last word you would have used to describe his personality. He had a problem with communication.

His mother's death, after roller-coaster months in which hopes had by turns been raised and dashed, had, seemingly, put Justin's life on indefinite hold. Michele, his sister two years his senior, was the only person with whom he felt able to have meaningful communication. His dad, Steve, tried hard to be both parents to Michele and Justin. But he had a demanding job that occupied him for long hours — and his own private wounds.

Michele's reaction to her mother's death probably holds the key that unlocks most doors in the house of mystery that was the next six years. With all she had in her, she had willed her gentle, Scottish mother to live. But in the icy, stone-hard days at the dawn of that awful year, the life dearest to her had been extinguished. *And she was angry*. Angry that despite every prayer and pious hope her mother was dead. Looking round for someone to blame, she saw only victims — her father, her brother, and two fond grandparents — so she took out her anger on God.

It had to be God, because her spade-bearded pastor

had shared with her the trauma of the roller-coaster months, had prayed fiercely and travelled miles daily to be at her mother's bedside. She couldn't blame *him*.

But when you're angry with God, what do you do? You find ways to hurt Him. You slam the door and shut Him out. You adopt a lifestyle that flies in the face of what you believe He stands for.

If you should have a badly-damaged brother, with an unlimited capacity for hurt but little capacity for anger, you might notice his beginning to mirror your rebellious patterns of behaviour.

That was, with the benefit of hindsight — and where is hindsight when you need it? — how Justin became the most unlikely rebel-on-autopilot.

When Steve found tubes in Justin's bedroom, he realized his son had been sniffing cannabis. Time for serious talking, he decided. Steve warned Justin of the dangers of drug-taking and how those who started with cannabis frequently went on to hard drugs. Much later, the suspicion dawned that the cannabis paraphernalia had been a cover for the real drug-of-choice, LSD. At all events, at 16, Justin fitted a lock on his bedroom door.

An aspect of Michele's rebellion was her involvement in the local Rave scene. Apart from a magazine available in some shops, there was no means of communication among those involved in 'the scene'. But no advertising seemed to be necessary when a Rave was in prospect. When one was planned everyone who needed to know knew. Though there were instances of Raves taking place in a well-known club — a one-time church with all the windows bricked up — those involved in the scene regarded these as anaemic affairs. Venues for all-night Raves were, more typically, disused warehouses or, better still, large, isolated farm buildings miles from anywhere.

On the night, as if by magic, thousands of young

people would turn up at the chosen venue in every kind of conveyance. Many of them after travelling long distances.

There was something addictive about Raves. Michele and her friends experienced it. And it was not simply the drugs, available from dealers much closer to home; it was the whole weird mix of pitch-black, strobed by photic lighting, the mindless, lyricless throb of the music interrupted only by the occasional shrieked obscenity. The whole brain-blasting experience that kept the devotees hooked. They lived from one Rave to the next, surviving in between whiles on Rave cassettes played full thunder — and on whatever drug they favoured.

Justin was still 15 when he, with his new friend Lee, accompanied Michele to his first Rave.

The Scene

As Justin was drawn more and more into the Rave scene, he hit the drugs harder. It is likely that he was trying a variety of drugs, but he was using LSD regularly. This came out only later. Justin's usual reclusive habits prevented anyone from spotting the tell-tale signs at first.

A Rave occupied one night. But those involved needed time to chill out (recover). Justin sometimes did not come home until two or three days after the night of the Rave. His cover was blown on the morning his father came downstairs to find the living room littered with zonked-out bodies, and he found some difficulty in picking his way over to the kitchen to make breakfast. On that occasion, Michele's and Justin's friends had chosen their home in which to 'crash'. However, they were to discover that morning that it was possible to recover rather more quickly than their accustomed three days! And then they had some awkward questions to answer . . . .

GCSEs, the tickets to ride the British economy, went by in a daze for Justin. Past promise and a high IQ were not reflected in the two passes he notched up. He left school. Most of the jobs he did were short-term, casual. He failed to hang on to the one or two jobs that did promise better prospects. Twice he launched into courses at the local college of further education, but both times dropped out after a few days. He became aware of an incapacity to stick at it for any length of time. He was antsy. Couldn't settle.

Justin was 18 in June 1994 when his father remarried. His new mother had a grown-up family and endeavoured to reintroduce stability — and regular, wholesome meals

— into his life. At first things began to improve. But the improvement tailed off when Michele's anger broadened its scope to include both father and stepmother.

Michele was by then 20 and, at her request, her father found her a neat little house to live in and she left home. Justin visited his sister regularly and their relationship was close.

It was a few days before Christmas when his own altered attitude became obvious. Until that time the father-son relationship had been warm. As far as Steve knew, this was still the case on the day he came home to an empty house after a long shift at work. While alone in the house, Justin had smashed a number of expensive items.

Soon after this, Justin moved to his sister's house. Once he had placed physical distance between himself and his father, the psychological distance grew. Justin began to hate his father. His behaviour became semiparanoid. He felt that everyone was talking about him, laughing at him, tearing him apart. A walk in the street became torture for him. He was convinced that every gust of laughter was at his expense.

At a later date, this would be seen as a significant development.

During this period there was nothing to prevent Justin's total involvement in the Rave scene. There was one Rave that, weeks later, Justin was able to describe with a degree of clarity unusual for him. Parts of it were also captured on video. Because of the photic lighting, the video appeared, at first, like a series of freeze-frames. In each frame someone who was clearly Justin was behaving in a most un-Justin-like way, flinging himself about to the tantric beat that thundered out from the great bank of amplifiers. Though he was gyrating in solitary isolation, it appeared that his customary inhibitions had completely disappeared in the electric, vibrating rhythm. It was as if he had stepped into another dimension; a dimension of an inner self that required drugs and the diabolic din to release it. He appeared beyond time, place and the awareness of others. The backdrop to his gyrating body was an endless mass of other gyrating bodies, all, seemingly, freed from the detritus of inhibition — brains vacuous, thinking facilities subsumed beneath the vibration of iterative, sense-numbing sounds.

As the video camera panned from Justin to the crowd, the freeze-frame effect ended. The camcorder was now penetrating the darkness, as well as the swift shafts of bright light. As it homed in on each solitary dancer, the body movements of every individual involved in this manic, catatonic seethe would have convinced many impartial observers that the participants were clinically insane. Other observers might have said that they were 'acting like aliens' or looked 'demented' or 'possessed'.

While he had lived at home, Justin had had cassettes of all the main Rave stars — The Prodigy, The Utah Saints, Moby, Mo Lester, M-Trance and The Shamen — but as his contorted body flung itself around in that techno-pagan bedlam the noise behind the amplifiers could have come from any source.

In his description later on, however, he would identify 'The Music Maker'; not a vocalist — there were no lyrics — but a central figure with a mike through which mindless directions (mostly obscene) were shouted above the clangour of dissonant sounds. Justin would also speak of two 'nun-like figures, dressed in black'. These figures were, it would appear, present at each Rave. Each time the women, elevated above the moon-struck mass of bodies, would fix their eyes on one individual. In that early spring Rave, Justin distinctly remembered that the wide-eyed gaze of one of them had been fixed on him throughout the night. A combination of drugs and acid house had enabled him to shed his inhibitions; but, nevertheless, he had not lost his awareness of that chilling stare. Other witnesses confirmed that Justin had been singled out that night.

When Michele moved with her boyfriend to a distant city, Justin faced a difficult situation. He hated his father to the extent that he could not speak his name, but he had nowhere to live. Fortunately, he had an understanding uncle and aunt who happily took him in. They grew determined to care for Justin as if he were their own child. It was his aunt who persuaded him to undertake one of his short-lived excursions into further education.

But soon old patterns re-emerged. He began spending his days in his bedroom watching TV, and avoiding communication with his uncle and aunt. On the occasions when it was necessary, Justin seemed at a loss, and each sentence demanded a superhuman effort. Nevertheless, he was pleasant; that was his nature. From time to time he would ask for money; his unemployment benefit rarely lasted more than a day or two after he had cashed his giro. His aunt, keen to establish a good relationship with him, willingly obliged. Build a good relationship, she believed, and she would be able to help him in all kinds of ways.

Then came the day when Michele and her boyfriend arrived to collect Justin. They were to take him to a Rave in a country area fifty miles distant. It was to celebrate Michele's 21st birthday. Exactly what drug Justin was given that night no one knows. But it was 'bad stuff'. Justin didn't get in to the Rave. He had a 'bad trip' and spent the night seriously ill in a car, not expecting to survive. He was ill for days. He did not return to the home of his uncle and aunt but stayed with his one friend, Lee. When he eventually did return, it was clear that he had had a devastating, perhaps horrifying, experience.

If Justin had been a non-talker before the birthday Rave, he was even less communicative afterwards. He spent his time alone, spoke hardly at all, and stared into middle distance.

Steve had visited his son during his stay with the understanding aunt and uncle. Occasionally, Justin had talked a little. Frequently, his father phoned and, even though it was clearly a painful experience, he forced words out of his son and re-established the lines of communication. Justin's hatred of his father was clearly decreasing.

But in proportion to the decrease in his hostility towards his father, his paranoia increased. This became a real source of concern to his aunt who arranged weekly visits to a psychiatrist. The interviews continued for some time and much was expected of them.

On Friday 9 June 1995, hopes were dashed. Uncle Zack found deep gashes down one of Justin's arms. Justin offered no explanation. Zack rang Steve and told him what had happened. Steve went to his son. They discussed the chemical and psychological damage caused by drugs. Justin admitted taking LSD for some years and said he wished he had quit a year previously. Steve asked Justin if he would like to come home. He immediately agreed and packed his things. There seemed to be a definite determination to change direction and end the habits that were both controlling and destroying him.

From Acid to Occult

That first night at home was a restless one. No one slept. Justin was back and forth to the bathroom all night.

Next day, Steve decided on a father-and-son day out. Justin willingly fell in with his plans. The air display seemed to distract him from whatever it was that was gnawing at his vitals. Relationships were healed. They returned home happy after a fun day out.

The atmosphere that day extended into the next. Steve was at work, but Justin related well to his stepmother, Natasha, spending the day reading and happily pitching in when meal-times came around. After Steve's return home, father and son collected the balance of Justin's belongings from his aunt and uncle's house with appropriate expressions of thanks. They then got stuck into preparations for a bonfire. This proved great fun and father and son videoed each other at work.

For some time, Justin had held down an evening office-cleaning job with a family friend, Chrissie. A young person herself, Chrissie was a born communicator. Justin responded to her well, but in the evenings following his return home he was totally lacking in energy, and candidly remarked upon the fact. He also complained to Chrissie of being 'light-headed'. He had decided to stop smoking, and that was assumed to be the explanation.

The bonfire proved a great family event with Natasha's son, only a little older than Justin, joining in the party. There was fun; video footage was shot, and Steve, who owned an excellent camera, took still pictures, too.

In the ensuing days a routine seemed to be establishing itself and a sort of normalcy reigned. Justin would spend his days doing jobs around the house, volunteering to wash a pile of dishes, cleaning his father's car and all the windows of the sizeable, detached house. Natasha noted that his bedroom was immaculate. He would have his tea at the dining table with Steve and Natasha and spend the evenings with the family watching TV. Best of all, he was making a valiant attempt to chat. He played some chess with his father, too.

Steve arranged for Justin to have an informal interview with a psychologist. He encouraged his son to open up and tell her all that was in his heart. The lady psychologist came to the house and stayed about twenty-five minutes. As soon as she left, so did Justin.

In the course of the evening, his aunt phoned to speak to him. Discovering that Justin was not at home, she panicked. Because of the new stability in Justin's routine, however, Natasha told her with some confidence that he had gone out on his bike because he felt embarrassed at having seen a psychologist and he would be back by 10. In the event, he arrived home at 10.10.

A meal was prepared which he ate cheerfully.

It was the following day that the first of a train of events that was to prove significant occurred. At 4 his father returned home from work and began sorting out papers in the living room, assuming that the house was empty. To his surprise, Justin suddenly burst out of his bedroom carrying his large portable TV, and marched down the stairs and across the sitting room to the patio door.

'Hey, what's up, Justin?' his father asked.

Justin replied, 'Don't try to stop me! There's something I've got to do.'

His father rushed towards him. But he was too late to prevent Justin from smashing his television against the brick wall with all his force. Justin was deeply distressed; that much was obvious.

Hurriedly, Justin retreated to the bathroom and his father went up after him. Though he would have welcomed an explanation of Justin's behaviour, he didn't press the point. Steve did, however, ask Justin how many times he had taken LSD. He was shocked by his reply: 'Hundreds of times.' But Justin had not, he said, taken any LSD since the Rave on the occasion of his sister's 21st birthday, nor had he listened to Rave music.

At this point, Justin went out for an hour or two on his bike. If it had not been clear before, it was certainly clear then that Justin needed professional help and needed it quickly. Steve phoned the doctor. 'Smashing things up, is he?' said the unhelpful medical man. 'You should tell the police!'

One option that had been discussed was that Justin should spend a period in a local psychiatric hospital. Someone close to the family had been helped by a period there, and was advocating this course of action as the appropriate one in Justin's case. Unfortunately, the very mention of the familiar name of this hospital was enough to feed Justin's paranoia. Hence, this was a topic that his father had endeavoured to steer clear of.

However, having watched his son smash to pieces, for no apparent reason, an expensive TV set, and having found no help from the family's doctor, Steve decided to telephone the psychiatric hospital. By this point, he was desperately concerned.

A senior psychologist at the psychiatric hospital listened carefully when Steve phoned to provide him with the details of the case. He advised Justin's remaining at home for the time being.

When Justin returned, he confessed to being depressed. He also vocalized his fear of being sent to a psychiatric hospital. The prospect appeared to terrify him.

By this time, Natasha's son, Michael, had been a part of the household for some months. Near to Justin's age, he made attempts to provide him with a source of friendship, but by then Justin's tolerance of normal social contact was limited, and he exposed himself to it as little as possible. Michael was, therefore, surprised one evening when he found on his bed, in a heap, Justin's expensive video games, worth some hundreds of pounds. With them was a little note saying that since he, Justin, had no further use for these games he hoped that Michael would appreciate them. The next time their paths crossed, Michael thanked Justin for the thought, but in view of the expense involved he couldn't possibly accept the gift; perhaps they could both make use of the games. Justin's response surprised Michael: 'So you're forcing me to have them, then?'

The next morning Justin made a phone call then went out for a short time on his bike. He returned with his friend Lee and they both went into the living room. Later, Natasha was surprised to find the boys just sitting in silence, not watching TV. Silence was an unusual state for Lee who was a great talker.

Not long afterwards, Justin, having been upstairs, brought down his hi-fi and re-entered the living room. Before much time had elapsed, he went out on his bike but was soon back.

Half an hour later, Lee walked through the kitchen where Natasha was working and said, 'I'm going now.' Natasha spoke to him for a short time about a recent illness he had had and then he went off. She presumed that Justin was still in the living room and that Lee had said his ten-fours before entering the kitchen.

Still believing this at lunchtime, Natasha went into the

living room with a tomato sandwich and a slice of blackberry and apple pie she had just baked. To her surprise, Justin was not there. She then jumped to the conclusion that he must have left the house at the same time as Lee, perhaps going through the garage, at the front of which he had left his bike.

She was pleased at the prospect of Justin spending the day with Lee. He hadn't seen Lee for some time, owing to his paranoia and she thought it a healthy sign that the two friends were together again.

By evening when Steve returned, there was still no Justin. At first it was assumed that he was spending the night at Lee's, and hence there was no panic. This had happened before, but not often.

On Saturday morning Steve phoned Lee's home. Lee sounded surprised; Justin was not there. Lee explained that on the previous day he had left *after* Justin. Indeed, Justin had left him sitting in the living room on his own for some time before he had decided to leave.

The next option was to contact Michele and her boyfriend to find out if Justin had cycled over to their flat. By this time, Michele lived some thirty miles distant and was not on the phone. In the course of the day, there was considerable concern. This intensified on the Saturday evening when Michele phoned and asked to speak to Justin. Justin was not at her home, either.

On Sunday morning Michele came over. The police had already been contacted and a photograph of Justin circulated.

On Sunday morning at 6.30 the doorbell rang. It was Justin. The door had been left unlocked all night in case he should come home, but he had not thought to check. There were no obvious signs of distress or ill health and, in response to his question, 'Is it OK if I come in?' Natasha said, 'Of course!'

Justin persisted, 'Are you sure it's OK?' Again he was reassured and was then asked if he wanted breakfast.

He declined, but when his father came downstairs he changed his mind.

Justin's explanation for his absence was a curious one. He had spent the time in the woods at Beltane Tower. Beltane Tower was a recently renovated folly, built by an eighteenth-century lord as an observatory. Though on National Trust land, the tower was a considerable distance from the seventeenth-century mansion that was the centre of the estate, and, indeed, from any other dwelling place. There were weird stories about it in the area, and the idea of spending time there by choice was odd in the extreme. Justin had, he said, gone away to think things through. He had kept dry by using bin liners, and had spent his time watching the wildlife. It was conjectured that he was still preoccupied with whatever impulse had caused him to smash his TV and that, in addition, he might have been hiding out to prevent any attempt to commit him to a psychiatric hospital.

After a light meal, Justin went to bed with a hot-water bottle. He got up when his sister and her boyfriend arrived at 11-ish. In the course of the day they spent together, Justin, Michele and Steve found themselves in the summer house. It was there that Justin began to open up about his problem. He said he had 'done something very bad' and, for the first time, began to speak about his 'voices' . . . .

The Voices

As Justin talked, inexplicable events — the smashing of the TV, the two days' absence in the woods — began to make a sort of sense.

But as Steve listened to his son, the explanation proved more disconcerting than any of his conjectures.

Justin had been hearing voices.

To him, the voices were entirely real and audible.

The voices came out of electronic equipment that was turned on.

It could be the hi-fi; it could be the TV, or the radio. . . . The speaker might be pumping out anything from heavy metal to the six o'clock news, but what Justin was hearing was a voice speaking very directly, he was sure, to him. . . .

It had all begun when he was living at the home of his aunt and uncle.

Justin had begun reading 'spooky' books. These books were of the sort that could be easily acquired from most bookshops and for which there is, at the present time, a significant demand. Satanism, occult phenomena and the like were the stock-in-trade of this genre of fiction.

One evening while watching TV at his aunt's, he had, without at first realizing what he was doing, drawn a series of occult symbols and an upside-down cross on a piece of paper. He had then, in response to a voice, circled the symbol and the inverted cross with blood taken from his own veins. He had not planned to do it. He didn't know why he had done it. Most surprising of all, he had been unaware that his memory contained the symbols he had drawn.

At a later stage, however, the symbols were traced to the appendix of one of the fictional books on Satanism. Justin was unaware that he had ever referred to this appendix.

As soon as he had completed his 'circle of blood', a voice speaking from the TV had said, 'If you are receptive to our powers you will feel a thump.' Immediately, Justin had felt a thump on his chest and had been terrified.

But this had been just the beginning.

'The voice' regularly spoke to Justin and acquired a tone of menace. The repeated threat that Justin believed he heard was that, if he did not act as instructed, either his father or his sister, or both, would be killed the following day. There was something about 'the voice' that had made Justin take the threats entirely seriously.

He was confirmed in his view when, one day, he was told that since he had been doing good deeds that day something evil would happen the next day: an earthquake.

On the following day, a major earthquake occurred in Greece.

Demands by 'the voice', at first, were idiotic rather than evil. One day he cashed his giro and bought himself a pair of pants. Later, it seemed as a test, the voice had 'instructed' him to burn his new pants *and* the rest of his money! This he had done. The threat, as always, had been that if he failed to comply Michele and his father would die in a car crash the following day. He didn't want them to die, so he obeyed.

The voice told him to have sex with Michele, and did so on more than one occasion. This, Justin refused to consider, regardless of the threat. But he did not openly defy the voice.

On another occasion, the voice told him that he was a

homosexual, that a friend of his was a homosexual, and that he must make contact with the friend and begin to practise homosexuality. The voice identified the friend by name. Justin had no doubts about his own heterosexual orientation; and later discovered that the friend identified was also a heterosexual and had had a girlfriend for some time.

From the first Justin had been convinced that 'the voice' that spoke to him was that of 'Ultimate Evil'. The instructions were too specific to be connected in any way with his drug habit. One instruction was that he must injure himself. He had inflicted wounds on his own arm. His uncle's discovery of these lacerations led to his decision that Justin should return to his father's care.

Another instruction had been that he must deprive himself of food, and that, if he ate, he must vomit it up. That was why he had been back and forth to the bathroom during the whole of the first night he had spent back at home. He had been forcing himself to vomit up his food.

Following Justin's return home, 'the voice' had insisted that he rid himself of all his possessions. He had destroyed his TV. He had tried to give away his video games. He had tried to persuade Lee to accept his hi-fi.

Eventually, 'the voice' had told him that he must leave home and spend time entirely alone in the woods beyond Beltane Tower . . . .

And his return from this enforced isolation had led to the strange outpouring of the whole saga in the summer house.

Steve listened to his son with deep concern.

As soon as he had him alone, adopting a Christian perspective, he began to speak of the danger and source of all occult and psychic phenomena. Justin accepted his explanation and its biblical basis.

For a day or two following the summer house discussion, 'the voice' was silent. Each day Steve would speak to Justin of spiritual things and use Scripture, not only to identify the nature of evil but to identify the Source of all good. Steve also told him to ignore the threats that accompanied the instructions; that nothing would happen to Michele or himself — and that if, by chance, it did, he, Justin, would not in any way be responsible, any more than he was responsible for the earthquake in Greece.

Whenever Justin spoke of 'the voices', he showed signs of extreme agitation. His father spent hours with him — on one occasion three hours at a stretch — talking things through, introducing the biblical perspective, reminding him of the all-powerful God. They spoke of Christ and of Calvary; and they prayed.

After some prayerful thought, Steve decided to introduce his son to a book that, for him, represented the clearest exposition of the Christian Gospel: *Steps to Christ*. When he presented the book to Justin, he explained its purpose and they had prayer together.

It became clear that Justin was eager for prayer. Hence, even after a game of chess and when there was no great spiritual crisis then current, father and son would kneel in prayer.

Justin spent the Monday of a fateful week energetically working on the garden. He cleaned his father's car, mowed the lawns and embarked on the daunting task of cutting the leylandi hedge. Nevertheless, both Steve and Natasha felt instinctively that they must not leave Justin on his own for any extended period.

At one o'clock Steve went to work. Natasha returned home, briefly, at 4 to check that all was well and then returned to work until 7.30.

When Justin came in from the garden, Michael, Natasha's son, kept him company. They sat together and watched television for about ten minutes. Then, suddenly, Justin shot out of the room when a strange, grotesque visage appeared on the screen.

Nevertheless, at 7.30 when Natasha returned from work, Justin was cheerful and sitting in the living room. He ate dinner and even attempted a few jokes. After the meal he went upstairs where Natasha noticed him lying on his bed reading *Steps to Christ*. When Steve returned from work at 10, he chatted with Justin for some time and, again, they prayed together.

Tuesday found Justin doing battle with the leylandi hedge again. He expressed enthusiasm for his work in the garden and responded positively to his father's suggestion that he should consider a course at a local horticultural college. Justin expressed the intention of making enquiries into it. He told his father that when he kept busy he didn't hear the voices.

On the Tuesday afternoon, he spent two or three hours with his grandmother, herself a loving, devout Christian. He felt able to unburden himself of his problems. She, too, heard the saga of the voices. She was warm and, as usual, he felt that she understood.

He spent the whole of the evening in his room alone. This seemed like a step backwards, but after his father's return at 10 the reason became clear. He had listened to the six o'clock news on the radio. And the voice had spoken again.

This time the voice had told him that hit men were out to get him. Believing this to be true, Justin had telephoned his grandmother. She had assured him that no hit men were going to get him. She had also checked to make sure that he was not in the house on his own.

Justin told his father that he had been terrified all

evening, looking out of the windows and making sure that all the doors were locked. Steve told him there were no hit men but, somehow, Justin could not accept that as a fact. Indeed, he insisted that his father fetch his Bible, place his hand on it and swear that no hit men were after him. Steve had to repeat this procedure a number of times before Justin was satisfied.

Everything then seemed OK. A late-night meal was eaten and father and son played chess. Before he went to bed, Justin asked Steve if it was humanly possible for him to have the next day (Wednesday) off work. Steve said he would telephone his firm the following morning but that he could foresee no problems about having a day off. Plans were made for father and son to have time out together.

Oaths on the Bible notwithstanding, Justin was still clearly uneasy about hit men and felt safer in his father's company. When they went to bed, they prayed by Justin's bedside. When the final amen was said, Justin commented, 'It's just like old times.'

As anticipated, the Wednesday morning telephone call to Steve's place of work received a helpful response. Father and son could spend the day together and decided that they would go out in the car. Justin asked if Lee could come too and Steve agreed.

Before they left, Justin prepared sandwiches and drinks for the three of them.

They drove to a tourist town some miles away and, in the course of looking at the attractions, bought chips and enjoyed them. From there they drove to a large reservoir used for water sports, one of the largest in the UK.

Happily, Justin and Lee stood by the lake, skimming stones across the water. Steve went to the car to fetch the drinks, and as he approached the two boys heard his son mutter, 'No, I'm not going to walk in there and take deep breaths. I'd rather lie across the railway line!'

Scarcely able to believe what he had heard, Steve asked, 'What was that?'

'Oh, nothing. You wouldn't understand.'

Afterwards, when the event came to be recounted, it was realized that, in all probability, that was the first time Justin had spoken back to the voice — and announced his intention of disobeying it.

This weird interlude was put behind them. Steve was determined that nothing would spoil the enjoyment of the day.

As they walked round the vast expanse of water, the three noted that a boat trip on a pleasure cruiser was about to set off. On an impulse, they bought tickets and went aboard. The boat was quite large and they sat on the upper deck, about twenty feet above the water-line. Justin and Lee sat together, Lee nearer to the water. Steve sat opposite Lee, near the water, and found himself absent-mindedly fingering the lifebuoy.

The sun was hot and the tour around the vast lake enjoyable.

Towards the end of the cruise, the captain spoke over the tannoy, inviting all to take their seats. At the instant he spoke, Steve was a few yards away, taking a photograph of Justin. He quickly returned to take his seat, but Justin deftly moved over to where he had been sitting.

A movement caught Steve's eye.

Justin had suddenly jumped on to the seat.

Steve leapt up immediately but, at that moment, Justin was on the railings and in the act of jumping.

Steve grabbed his legs but the force of his heavy body was such that the legs slipped out of the father's grasp . . . .

Steve threw out the lifebuoy. Justin made no attempt to take hold of it.

He had been a strong swimmer. But the second he touched the water he vanished.

Steve shouted to the captain: 'My son's jumped overboard!'

Acting swiftly, the captain began to turn the boat.

Later, witnesses would say that Justin had dropped through the water as a stone falls through air.

Nearby, frogmen were working on a project. In seconds, they went to the rescue.

The reservoir was deep. It took them four hours to locate the body and haul it to the surface. It was bloated with water. Justin's watch had stopped at 3.51, the second he hit the water.

The voice — perhaps speaking through the tannoy — had spoken for the last time.

The Inquest

The Coroner's verdict was: 'Suicide by drowning.' But that was the easy part. The inquest within the family was far more searching and painful.

The more unexpected the death, the greater the grief. There were so many things they had to say to one another. Sadly, but inevitably, unwise things were said; assertions made; 'blame' apportioned. As they thought of Justin, there were so many severed threads, like the loose ends of unfinished conversations. There were volumes of 'if onlys'.

After Justin's body had been recovered, Natasha rang Michele. Suddenly she found she could not tell her what had happened and said, 'Please come over.' It was said in such a tone that Michele came over right away.

Breaking the news to Grandmother was quite an assignment. First she had lost her daughter, Justin's mother. One year to the day before Justin's death, her husband, a victim of Alzheimer's disease, had wandered off and never returned; and there had been two months of insupportable uncertainty until his body was recovered by a farmer harvesting his wheat field. Now she was being told that her grandson had committed suicide . . . .

Michele was sorrow-torn, inconsolable; there were no words to describe her depth of feeling.

Steve was so unnerved and heartbroken that some feared for him. There had been a long period of night-and-day anxiety on Justin's behalf. But in the two weeks preceding his death all the indicators had been that Justin was on the up. He had quit drugs, emancipated himself from the Rave scene that had led him into drugs and their effects, had sought to escape the voices (though he had not ceased to fear them) and, with his father, had explored and accepted the Bible's perspective on the occult. Most important of all, he had prayed with his father *and* begun to fight his way back to faith.

The picture that repeatedly flashed into Steve's mind was of Justin, having jumped into the water, slicing through the surface — *and straight down*. Someone suggested that it had looked as if unseen hands were pulling the nearly-19-year-old boy downwards. Certain it was that there had been no struggle and he had never resurfaced.

Inevitably, the funeral was an ordeal that had to be lived through. But the pastor — who, himself, had hit the alcohol and Rock scene before coming to Christ — was able to say things that meant something, not just to the immediate family but to the cross-section of the Rave scene that turned up at church. The account of Justin's death had been in the newspapers.

As it turned out, the Rave crowd had the last word. They bought space in the newspaper and had this note inserted:

'To Justin, the greatest little Raver of them all. Rave on!'

It got back to the family that Justin's suicide had made him a hero with the Rave crowd. The brand of eighties Hard Rock out of which Rave had evolved in the nineties had been nihilistic and obsessed with death. Major figures in the hard rock scene, mentors to millions, had killed themselves and thereby achieved a doubtful 'immortality'. Self-destruction seemed to be the logical, desired end of the hate-ridden, love-empty, wilderness-bleak lifestyle they lived and lauded. And Justin had destroyed himself.

Or had he?

This was the problem churning up Steve and Michele. Those voices. Were they chemically induced? Were they echoes from a Freudian subconscious? If so, why had their demands been so specific and their threats so menacing, repetitive and explicit? Perhaps the clue was in how they had begun: the occult symbols, the ring of blood, the blow to the chest.

We have undertaken an investigation of the three forces that had given the 'voices' access to Justin's life — and such apparent power to drive it:

- Drugs
- The heavy Rock-Rave scene
- The sinister power of the occult which, in a hundred ways, seeks to gatecrash, shape and control the lives of the young.

'Suicide by drowning' was a satisfactory coroner's verdict. But it begged so many questions, and the answers to those questions lie in three sinister, threatening lines of enquiry. If the inquest into the three forces that cut short the promising life of Justin — drugs, Rock-Rave, and the occult — could be conducted with some vigour, then a more satisfactory verdict might be brought in.

Justin is dead. We need to identify his killers. They have struck again, repeatedly. They will continue to strike, perhaps with increasing frequency, until we are successful in increasing awareness of them. Only through such awareness can we curb their mind-warping, body-wasting, life-destroying progress.

Getting into Drugs

Kurt Cobain came as close as any popular musician to being a symbol of the nineties generation. The 27-year-old leader of the American 'grunge trio', Nirvana, shot himself at his home near Seattle on 23 July 1993. 'The tidal wave of acclaim which turned a scruffy small-town punk band into the most internationally-influential rock act of recent years had to do with more than just music,' wrote *The Times* leader. 'The mixture of raving naïvety and screaming rage which made Nirvana's sound so distinctive struck a chord with millions to whom growing up in the material world of the 1980s had been a disorientating experience . . . .'

Cobain was to 'the slackers' what Sid Vicious was to the punks, and Jim Morrison was to the hippies — a glamorous epitome of the self-destructive victim figure.

But how did Cobain get there?

He had been a heroin addict since 1992. There had been a series of crises in which he was admitted to hospital, the result of overdosing on alcohol and barbiturates. The anger of his brand of rock was often compared with the anger of the Sex Pistols of the late seventies. In fact, Cobain's brand of anger, evidenced in offstage behaviour, left the Sex Pistols trailing miles behind. A sympathetic biographer quotes him as saying, 'When people muck me about, I just can't help but want to beat them to death.' The beatings he sought to hand out to those who crossed him — at rehearsals, at concerts, at parties — were in dead earnest. He was trying to commit murder. And he would have succeeded on a number of occasions had not his assailant (or his assailant's friends) proved to have superior strength; or had his own minders not hauled him off in time.

'Kurt Cobain's suicide is deeply troubling for the generation he was supposed to represent,' wrote *The Times* man. 'When the spokesman for his generation blows his head off, what is the generation supposed to think?'

An interview with Cobain's widow, Love, in *Vox* (May/June 1995), gives an important insight into life with a drug-sodden icon.

On the day Love gave birth to their daughter Frances, Cobain was on a morphine drip. *Vox* asked Love what it was going to be like for Frances to grow up 'in the shadow of her famous father's shotgun blast'. Love was not overly concerned about that; she was training her 3-year-old to 'honour my husband's spirit'. Love is a New Ager, Tibetan Buddhist branch. Cobain's ashes are divided among her bedroom Buddha, her living room altar, and a shrine in India (specially blessed by the Dalai Lama). While Love was giving birth to Frances, Cobain had been in another hospital. An army of doctors and nurses notwithstanding, he had arranged for a dealer 'to come and stick a needle in the IV'. There followed a crisis that completely overshadowed the birth of his daughter. The injection caused an overdose and, in the words of his wife, Cobain 'totally died'. 'He would die all the time. Some people OD. I never ODed ever,' she continued. 'I've gotten really *** blasto, but instead of ODing I end up screaming and running round naked and getting hysterical, cutting my arms . . . you know, crazy ***. But I have never fallen on the floor blue,' she concluded.

With the *Vox* reporter looking on, Love began to distract 3-year-old Frances by shuffling photographs in front of her and asking her to identify the people on them. '*Mummy!*' said Frances triumphantly. 'And who's that?' 'Daddy!' In fact, Frances had pointed to Eric Nies of The Grind, 'mistaking one MTV icon for another'.

Cobain had got his kicks hanging out with dealers. His wife said he was a 'gobbler'. 'If you had acid, he'd take acid. If you had mushrooms, he'd take mushrooms. When it came to drugs, he was abusive in a very intensive way. If there were forty pills, he'd take forty pills, instead of taking two pills and making it last a month. He took eight Prozacs once, and he got furiously sick . . . .'

On a number of occasions Love had found her husband by the side of the bed 'dead, blood coming out of his nostrils'. His comas would last between two and four days. What happened on 23 July 1993 was that Cobain, in the words of his wife, 'totally died'.

The association between Rock and the drug culture is an old one. It is, in fact, possible to date it to the 1965-6 watershed in the career of the Beatles. This watershed, in turn, was influenced by the hot breath of India — from which they imported both drugs and New Age religion — and Professor Timothy Leary, author of *The Psychedelic Reader* and *The Psychedelic Experience*. Between them the Beatles and Professor Leary were to be the Pied Pipers of the sixties generation. When Leary died in March 1996, Alistair Cook made him the subject of the BBC's 'Letter from America' for the week. Examining Leary's career in some detail, Cook, uncharacteristically hostile, laid at Leary's door much of what is evil in contemporary society.

Following the Beatles' return from India, John Lennon was in a studio singing a lyric made up of lines from Timothy Leary's version of the sacred text: *The Tibetan Book of the Dead*. Paul McCartney was telling the press: 'God isn't in a pill but (LSD) explained the mystery of life. It was a religious experience.'

The twin influences of Hinduism with a Western face and LSD totally changed the nature of popular music in the West. The Beatles had left for India at their 'scream-age' peak. When they returned, they were writing lyrics based on Hindu texts.

The experience of the Beatles was to be repeated in the lives of the most influential rock musicians of the sixties. Even Brian Wilson of the Beach Boys was soon saying, 'My experience of God came from acid . . . .' There was a boom in Zen Buddhism, Hinduism and other forms of pagan religion/magic. But, at this stage, the real 'magic' ingredient was the hallucinogen LSD, commonly referred to as 'acid'.

By the end of 1967, most rock musicians were on it — John Lennon, Paul McCartney, George Harrison, Mick Jagger, Keith Richards, Brian Jones, Pete Townsend, Steve Winwood, Brian Wilson, Donovan, Cat Stevens, Jim Morrison, Eric Clapton and Jimi Hendrix among them. In his history of rock,[1] Steve Turner writes: 'This was the Damascus Road tablet. People started out on trips as hard-nosed materialists after a bit of fun, and emerged with their egos ripped and mauled, unsure at first whether they'd seen God or whether they were god.'

There was just enough publicity in the media to associate drugs with glamorous pop people, but insufficient to make the many-headed youthful multitude aware of the 'bad trips' and 'bummers' that went with addiction. After his first 'trip', Paul McCartney felt 'love and truth'. But in his many trips, Rolling Stone Brian Jones saw nothing but demons and monsters!

Early on in his exposure to LSD (1965), John Lennon admitted to having been 'pretty stoned for a month or two', a period during which he believed he was 'being pursued by the devil'. A decade later, Lennon, nevertheless, boasted that he'd been on over a thousand trips.

Timothy Leary wrote his books before his expulsion as a Harvard University professor. He interpreted the effects of LSD in quasi-religious terms. LSD was, he said, more than a means of 'spiritual insight'; it was 'the deepest religious experience of my life'. He conducted an experiment with a group of theological students; 90 per cent of them later claimed to have had 'a mystical experience'. He founded the League of Spiritual Discovery which campaigned for LSD to be recognized as a 'legal sacrament'.

'Drugs', Professor Leary told a gathering of psychologists in Philadelphia, 'are the religion of the twenty-first century. Pursuing the religious life today without using psychedelic drugs is like studying astronomy with the naked eye.' He equated his drug 'visions' with the 'soma' mentioned in the Vedic scriptures, foundational to Hinduism. Drugs, argued Leary, had always been the Hindu's route to meditation. In shamanistic religions, the shaman (a pagan high priest who dealt with the gods on behalf of his tribe) would, said Leary, use both drugs and music to create the mental state to make possible contact with the spirit world.

Rock musicians were, said Leary, 'the philosopher poets of the new religion'. He called the Beatles, in particular, 'the four evangelists'.

Leary's message: Turn on to LSD; tune in to the new consciousness; drop out of straight society. John Lennon and Jimi Hendrix were as close to Leary and to his views as anyone in the period. Together, this triumvirate transformed the rock scene and made the rock scene and the drug scene synonymous between 1965 and 67.

It was not until 1977 that the term 'New Age movement' gained currency. Nevertheless, by the early seventies, Leary's League of Spiritual Discovery was asserting that the 'all one' experience was only possible through LSD use. 'Teenage children', wrote Leary, 'mutate through acid up to the higher level of existence.' Through LSD, he continued, man could make an evolutionary leap to a near-perfect state.

The pop people spoke, and the multitudes listened — and then went away to find the vaunted experience through the magic chemical.

When the Beatles split, there were plenty of others to preach the mind-blowing, life-destroying message. Among them was Grateful Dead. With many other groups, Grateful Dead performed at the open-air rock festivals in which the new paganism was lyricised — and practised: New Age religion and freely available hard drugs.

The contents of Kurt Cobain's suicide note were never made public. But many times, to massive audiences, he had said: 'I hate myself and I want to die.'

The suicide of a world-renowned rock star jolted the international press into an examination of 'the lifestyle' he advocated. *The Times* published the lyric of Cobain's inflammatory song: 'Rape me, Rape me, my friend/ Waste me, taste me, my friend.' Emma Forrest concluded her examination of the Cobain style: 'Cobain sat, willing to be ravished, begging for death to take him. When death refused to violate him, he violated death.'

Within days Forrest was reporting the disappearance and subsequent death of Richard 'Richey' James Edwards, guitarist and lyricist with the Manic Street Preachers. His abandoned car was found by the Severn Bridge. Writing his obituary for *Melody Maker*, Forrest observed: 'Everybody wants a messiah — from Kurt Cobain to Forrest Gump.'

It was then that the spate of teenage suicides began . . . .

---

[1]Steve Turner, *Hungry for Heaven: Rock and Roll the Search for Redemption* (Hodder, 1994 edition) pages 49, 50.

Death Music

'Kurt Cobain kills himself, Richey James from the Manic Street Preachers vanishes . . . ; young fans notice,' writes Libby Purves in *The Times*, 13 May 1995. 'The news reports another overdose after bullying, or before exams, another rescue from a railway bridge. And the children, streetwise and troubled, think their thoughts and ask their questions,' she concludes.

One authority[1] made a direct connection between the alarming rise in the suicide rate among teenagers and the deaths of Kurt Cobain and Richey James. Looking at the broader trend, the same authority wrote: 'Among young men suicide has risen by 71 per cent over the past decade (1985-95).' Conclusion? While the short-term rise resulted from two high-profile rock suicides, for the explanation of the longer-term rise we must examine a more basic trend shaping teenage thinking . . . .

Glenda Cooper has written: 'In reality, the most Cobain and James achieved was to make suicide slightly more socially acceptable. . . . The growth in teenagers — and teenage boys — killing themselves had begun long before that.'

Rock star deaths in unusual circumstances — from murder through drugs overdose to AIDS — have been numerous. John Lennon, Freddie Mercury, Brian Jones, Elvis Presley, Jimi Hendrix, Janis Joplin and Keith Moon, all had high-profile deaths that placed them in a sort of pantheon. Not long after they were joined by Kurt Cobain, Ian Curtis of the inappropriately named Joy Division hanged himself in his home. Richard Manuel of The Band, Till Ambers of Badfinger, and soloists Phil Ochs, Pete Ham and Tom Evans all hanged themselves. While not all of these suiciders had large cult followings, two or three did. And the teenage press, by the way that it reported the suicides and hyped their careers-in-retrospect, lent a ghoulish glamour to their deaths.

Steve Butler from the Samaritans visited Year 9 of a London Comprehensive to talk about suicide awareness. Perhaps in an effort to shock, he went into details about the death of a girl who had jumped off a railway bridge onto the 25,000-volt power cable. However, in the discussion that followed his talk, he discovered that the majority of his audience not only empathized with the suiciders, but had seriously contemplated taking their own lives at one time or another. On the first anniversary of Kurt Cobain's death, British pop paper *Melody Maker* received so many desperate letters from teenagers that they broke confidentiality, and handed them all over to the Samaritans who organized a contact group.

Professor Michael Rutter has demonstrated that disorders associated with suicide are increasing in Western society. Peter Wilson, a psychiatrist and a director of the children's mental health charity Young Minds, says that though suicide before puberty is rare, puberty is getting earlier. Despite the difficulties in studying puberty and post-puberty suicides — 'the coroner stretches doubt to protect the family' — the sharp rise since the mid-eighties is impossible to disguise in the national statistics of the USA, the UK and the majority of developed European countries.

Numerous features have appeared in US and European newspapers analysing the trend. Their conclusions are legion and none is to be discounted. Among them are the pressures of puberty in a sexually-charged culture, the disintegration of the family, the decline in the influence of Christianity, the impact of unemployment — and

the influence of the media. The glamorization of super-
star deaths in the teenage press takes its share of the
blame, as does the sense of inadequacy resultant from
media lionization of the glitzy success of the few.[2]

Some newspaper analyses toss in a reference to 'morbid trends in fringe/popular music' or 'the undue influence of the apparent death-wish in the lyrics of "heavy
metal", "death metal" and "thrash and rave" bands'.

So what evidence *is* there of a death obsession in
heavy metal and rave music?

Vivienne James, 19, has undertaken extensive research
into this theme, and chosen to contribute her findings to
this book.

It was a lyric from Metallica that first put Vivienne
onto a possible connection between heavy metal and the
spate of suicides:

> *Life it seems will fade away*
> *Drifting further every day*
> *Getting lost within yourself*
> *Nothing matters, no one else.*
> *I have lost the will to live*
> *Simply nothing more to give*
> *There is nothing more for me*
> *I need the end to set me free.*

Vivienne analysed twenty-six different heavy metal
magazines on sale in a single retail outlet. A sampling of
what she found will suffice. In one magazine (RAW No.
117), Vivienne found the following: 310 references to
death; 107 references to drugs; 44 references to Satan.

In these magazines, Vivienne found whole acreages of
obscene language which lauded death, perverted sex and
majored on blasphemy. An article on the group Death
Metal entitled 'Deicide' cited Glen Benton as saying: 'I
would like to kill all Christians; I worship Satan.' An

inverted cross, the most popular satanic symbol, was branded into his forehead and he wore chains round his neck, each link inscribed with an occult symbol. Death obsession, satanism, and perverted sex: a heady brew.

At least two young people committed suicide after listening to Ozzy Osbourne's 'Suicide Solution'.

The obsession-with-death theme and the anti-Christian theme were frequently one and the same. One analysis traces it to the 1965-66 Beatles' watershed, after which Lennon in particular went out of his way to show contempt towards Christianity, while credulously and un-critically absorbing the large-sounding (but often mean-ingless) utterances of the gurus and the age-old beliefs of Hinduism.[3]

In the eighties 'Material Girl' Madonna had used a small church as the setting for her controversial 'Like a Prayer' video (1989) in which, in an ecstasy of piety and erotic attraction, she had first kissed the feet of an image, and then magically developed the stigmata. The death-element in her performances has tended to be a gory, almost slobberingly sadistic delight in the wounds of crucifixion.

The nineties brought performers like Jesus Jones, Faith no More, The Jesus and Mary Chain, and MC 900 FT Jesus. Again the death-and-murder theme has re-curred. MC 900 almost crooned a ditty about 'the killer inside me'. The heavy metal group Metallica combined lyrics glamorizing death, with others bearing titles such as 'The God that Failed'. The rock group Guns 'N' Roses, at one time the most idolized musicians in the world, in the USA alone sold twelve million copies of their album 'Appetite for Destruction' (that is, nearly half US teenagers had one).

In November 1991 research undertaken by the US National Coalition on Television Violence examined 750 music videos featured on cable and broadcast television. They found an astonishing average of twenty acts of extreme violence per hour. On MTV, by far the most popular and influential of the big music networks, the situation proved even worse; there were twenty-eight instances of violent imagery in an hour of programming. After their weeks of analysis, the NCTV acknowledged that in choosing to screen the videos for violence they might well have made a mistake. The more pervasive atmosphere had been one of death. In the preamble to their report they acknowledged that the average age of the viewer of music videos on TV was somewhere between 14 and 16.[4]

The videos chosen for analysis by the NCTV were from the mainstream of popular culture. On the fringes of the rock world (though still selling to millions of fans) were lyrics from 'rebel' groups. These were far more grotesque in their violence-and-death imagery. The theme of the lyric 'Your Mommy's Dead' from Grammy-nominated Los Angeles' band Suicidal Tendencies was — the dismemberment of somebody's mother!

'Gangster Rap' included the same grotesque violence/death images. Indeed, some of the strongest voices condemning this imagery in contemporary music have come from the Black community. Leonard Pitts, writing in *The Miami Herald*, asked his readers: 'Maybe I'm crazy, but am I the only one who thinks it obscene that this popular new genre was born out of the exploitation of a sick violence that has wrecked thousands of lives? I'm not saying that Gangster Rap causes this tragedy, but that it legitimizes it.'

US Vice-president Al Gore and his wife, in public speeches, have stressed the connection between the brutal themes in contemporary music and the increasingly unstable and menacing atmosphere at rock concerts. Since the mid-eighties, at least thirty rock and rap enthusiasts have died in concert-related violence, while well over a hundred have suffered serious injury. 'With albums like ''Death Certificate'' who can be surprised?' asked Mrs Gore. 'It was direct incitement to violence against the Korean community in Los Angeles. Six months after the record's release angry crowds of rioters did as the song recommended — burnt the stores of the Koreans — several hundred Korean American shops were torched in the LA disturbances.'

Vincent from the band Morbid Angels says, 'I would kill someone and not think twice about it.' One *Melody Maker* analysis of the output of the group My Dying Bride concluded with: 'This is music for manic depressives, nooses at the ready, here we go!'

The UK's newspaper-for-the-scholars, *The Independent on Sunday*, published special supplements in January and February 1996 on what it saw as the three major obsessions in popular culture: Sex, drugs, rock. In its supplement on rock[5] the word *nihilistic* was repeatedly used to describe the output and 'philosophy' of the most influential rock bands.

Pause for definition.

Nihilism. n. total rejection of current religious beliefs or moral principles. *Shorter Oxford English Dictionary*.

The death-obsession can be seen as the extreme of this endorsement of all forms of antisocial behaviour. The lyrics of The Bends, Radiohead, Grateful Dead, The Shamen, Nirvana, Soundgarden and Pearl Jam provided *The Independent's* team of writers with more than enough material to illustrate their point. Another heavy British newspaper had already trawled through the lyrics of the previous fifteen years and traced the *nihilistic* theme.[6] David Bowie had written a song telling a lover in admiring terms that she was a 'rock and roll suicide', and recorded a song entitled 'My Death'. A Sheffield band called Cabaret Voltaire had issued a single called 'Why kill time when you can kill yourself?' A nihilistic New York group had actually called itself Suicide.

US News and World Report[7] homes in on heavy metal music which it describes as 'teenage nihilism, complete with liberal doses of violent sex and occasional thoughts of suicide'. *Time* magazine reported: 'Metal musicians play to the alienated fantasies of the mostly white, young and male audience by portraying themselves as disillusioned outsiders who have turned their backs on a corrupt civilization.'

The base line on the contemporary scene — whether we call it Rave, Festy-Rave, Techno Pagan, Acid House, Hit House, Tribal, Trance, or Post Punk — is that it is antisocial and obsessed by death.

It takes all sorts to *un*make a world.

But the world comes in units of one. Individuals. And the individuals targeted and affected by the latest wave of sound and fury are, because of the age bracket to which they belong, the most vulnerable and impressionable in society.

Justin died in June 1995, at the height of the influence of this alternative culture and, judging by the 'epitaph' they had printed in the newspaper, we conclude that they judged his death a triumph. Some triumph! A life of promise ended needlessly, pointlessly. Either Professor Leary's LSD-induced 'new consciousness' completely eluded Justin, or 'new consciousness' is a euphemism for death.

---

[1] *The Observer*, 26 March 1995. [2] *The Times*, 13 May 1995. [3] *The Mail on Sunday*, 13 October 1996; *The Sunday Times*, 28 February 1993. [4] Michael Medved 'The Corruption of Rock', *The Sunday Times*, 28 February 1993; Bob and Gretchen Passantino, *When the Devil Dares Your Kids*, (Eagle, 1996), pages 108-114, 118, 119. [5] *The Independent on Sunday*, 21 January 1996. [6] *The Observer*, 26 March 1995. [7] Cited in *The Independent on Sunday*, 4 February 1996.

Know the Score

Leah Betts, a glamorous Essex teenager, died tragically after a Rave party.

She was a victim of one of the so-called 'designer drugs' — ecstasy — and her death brought home to the UK population the pressures teenagers are under to 'do drugs'.

Peer pressure is fierce, at school, college, recreational centres, night clubs — but is never greater than at parties. There the pusher can add an extra line to his patter: 'Celebrate . . . it doesn't happen every day . . . get a life!'

Investigations by journalists have proved that ecstasy, LSD and heroin are widely available in every community. LSD, or acid, they have noted, is common because it is cheap.[1]

Six months too late for Justin, the British government announced an advertising campaign with the slogan, 'Know the score'. Its purpose: to help people discover the truth about the effects of drugs. 'Pushers claim that they deliver happiness,' reads the hand-out. 'This pamphlet reveals what they do not say — that the drugs can cause mental illness, kidney failure and death.'

But drugs and rock have been inextricably mixed for thirty years. Timothy Leary argued that LSD was the 'sacramental catalyst' to 'the new consciousness. . . . Turn on, tune in, and drop out.' Behind the slogan, Leary's books provided the theory. It was not Leary's theory, however, but the Beatles' example that led the first rock generation into drug abuse.

Tripping on LSD. When the Beatles returned from India in the mid-sixties, they behaved as if they had had some sort of 'conversion' experience. The utterances of Lennon and McCartney soon made it clear that the conversion had nothing to do with Christianity and that the road ended at the Ganges, not at Damascus. LSD, they argued, showed a truth hidden from the people: that creation was one massive, heavenly divinity. Lennon said, 'We're all God. I'm not a god, nor the God, but we're all potentially divine.' Before long, Lennon was claiming to have had over 1,000 'trips'. Monotheistic religions such as Islam, Judaism and Christianity were out; but Hinduism, Buddhism, occult doctrines and New Age were in.

LSD had, in fact, been discovered by a Swiss biochemist working with rye fungus. There had been secret experiments in the USA during the fifties. It was on the street by 1961, and 25,000 Americans were estimated to have tried it by 1962. In 1966 it was made illegal in both the US and the UK. Nevertheless, four years later it was reckoned that 5 million Americans had tried it.

Meanwhile, it had transformed the rock scene. Drug culture became implicit in many of the lyrics. Beyond that, distorted sounds and blurred album photographs suggested messages from initiates. Just as the Gnostics had believed that there were those who had received 'gnosis' (knowledge) and those who hadn't, the 'acid heads' assumed superiority over the 'straights' who had not 'turned on'.

'The subject feels he knows, essentially, everything there is to know,' wrote William Braden. 'He knows ultimate truth. And what's more, he knows that he knows it. Yet this sense of authority cannot be verbalized because the experience is a whole which cannot be divided.'[2] Paul McCartney echoed this; he had been introduced to 'the mystery of life' but it was 'impossible to put it into words'.

Tripping on LSD became the entry ticket to the rock scene. The music of Jimi Hendrix, The Grateful Dead, and Cream resonated and shimmered with 'LSD consciousness'.

By the early seventies, rock had become the jump start for the psychedelic (LSD) experience.

Acid casualties. Superficially, the 'psychedelic experience' was all naïvety; 'flower power', love-ins, peace and a jargon language that identified all initiates. But below the surface was the usual dark world of infected syringes, unexplained deaths, underworld pushers, organized crime, sexually-transmitted diseases, and not-spoken-about victims by the skip-load. If stories circulated about 'bad trips' or 'bummers' and minds that had never returned, they were dismissed as 'acid casualties'.

But as the 'acid casualties' mounted there was a reaction. John Lennon turned on Timothy Leary. George Harrison, after a much-publicized visit to the Haight-Ashbury district of San Francisco where the psychedelic culture had originated, said, 'It was just lots of dirty people lying around on the floor . . . .' McCartney said, 'They say it will lead to expanded consciousness, that love will flow from you. It doesn't work . . . .'

The Beatles, at least, had abandoned the chemicals; but they were still heavily into Eastern spirito-babble and gurus.

But, having shoved LSD into the headlines, the Beatles found that no one was listening when they condemned it. For many, LSD was the key catalyst to the cocktail that was Hinduism-with-a-Western-face that coloured popular culture.

LSD was mass-produced in the seventies. Pete Townsend said, 'Acid has happened, and the acceleration of spiritual thinking was obviously the purpose for it.' George Harrison conceded: 'Acid was the key that opened the door.' Even The Moody Blues were into LSD. The Grateful Dead were synonymous with the LSD experience.

For some seventies' groups, LSD was doing more than opening the door to a vague 'psychedelic experience'. It was 'disarranging minds by hauling demons and monsters from what appeared to be the depths of the sub-conscious . . . '.[3] Eric Clapton recalls hallucinating on stage in San Francisco while playing with the group Cream, 'his guitar apparently resonating with the spirit world . . . '.[4]

By the mid-seventies, rock figures were beginning to look back on the psychedelic experience — 'make love not war' — as decidedly namby-pamby. It had been replaced by an obsession with personalized evil. Jerry Garcia of The Grateful Dead testified that on LSD he had seen things that were 'frighteningly evil'. The Rolling Stones saw the same things but professed to have been fascinated rather than frightened.[5] Early Led Zeppelin music was oppressively heavy with the atmosphere of evil.

Books emerged on the Manson murders. It became evident that Charles Manson had used both the ego-destroying techniques of Eastern religion and hallucinogenic drugs to achieve mind-control of his followers.

When an attempt was made to transplant the Woodstock pop festival to California — at Altamont — a section of the crowd, heavy on LSD, produced such violent and bloody behaviour that even Leary himself must have begun to experience some self-doubt.

Routes to the paranormal. By the late seventies, the New Age movement in its various manifestations was having a major influence on popular culture. Hatha yoga, the various forms of meditation, and LSD were each viewed as routes to the gamut of paranormal experiences open to the New Ager. Singer/song-writer — and LSD-taker — John Anderson claimed to have experienced 'astral travelling' (an out-of-body experience). Those who viewed the New Age movement as a revival of the wisdom and lore of ancient civilizations saw all hallucinogenic drugs as aids to 'enlightenment', Buddhist-style.

Degrees of 'Rock'. As the eighties progressed, it became possible to categorize what had formerly been known as 'Rock' and, in doing so, to become aware of an easily-discernible hardening process, culminating in Rave.

ROCK — HARD ROCK — HEAVY METAL — KERRANG — THRASH METAL — RAVE.

Rock, Hard Rock and Heavy Metal contain lyrics. Kerrang, Thrash Metal and Rave are just wild, iterative, mind-burstingly loud noises with no obvious lyrics but, according to some sources, containing subliminal messages here and there. The drug scene and the rock scene were inextricably intermixed right across the spectrum. However, Thrash Metal and Rave were generally viewed as physically impossible without illegal drugs.

On 21 January 1996, *The Independent on Sunday* published a major supplement on the part played by drugs in popular culture. It included a survey conducted by Mori. A sample aged 16-54 had been presented with a list of drugs — LSD, alcohol, amphetamines, cannabis, cocaine, crack, ecstasy, glue, heroin, magic mushrooms, methadone, PCP, temazepam and cigarettes — and asked which ones they had heard of/tried/would consider acceptable for others to take/were currently taking.

Before presenting the picture, *The Independent* entered a caveat. The family physician is believed to accept the following as a rule of thumb; 'If a patient tells you how much he drinks a week, double it. When he tells you how often he has sex, halve it.' Sex — in most forms at least — and alcohol were legal, said *The Independent*. How much more difficult was it to establish a true picture with regard to the usage and abusage of drugs . . . ?

Drug abuse emerged, almost exclusively, as a youth activity with a cut-off point around the age of 35. There was, however, a deep generational schism in the way that drug use was regarded. Drug experimentation peaked among 20-24-year-olds. Twenty-one per cent admitted to having used LSD, 28 per cent speed, 45 per cent cannabis, 12 per cent ecstasy, and 5 per cent magic mushrooms.

The author of *Dope Girls*, a book that examines the birth of the British underground drug scene, points out an interesting distinction made by the drug abusers themselves. 'It was OK to take drugs that supposedly expanded your consciousness like cannabis and LSD,' she wrote. 'But stimulants like cocaine and amphetamines were seen as anti-social.'

Dope Girls was published in the mid-eighties. *The Independent* recorded a seismic shift in attitudes between the mid-eighties and the mid-nineties. 'Rave culture has eradicated all such rules and reservations,' commented the team of journalists. 'Few substances are now viewed as out of bounds or un-hip. Ten years ago all drugs were perceived as powerful substances that controlled the taker and dominated his or her lifestyle. Now the opposite seems to be true — and increasingly so . . . .'

The Independent examined the strong association between the drug culture and the rock scene. The lyrics of *Casey Jones* by The Grateful Dead were somehow symbolic: 'Drive that train/high on cocaine/Casey Jones you'd better watch your speed . . . .'

Drugs digest. A pop culture sodden with drugs is bound to have victims. Some victims will be like Leah Betts; more or less instant death as a result of a single dose of their drug-of-choice. Then there are the victims whose deaths come more slowly by way of ruined lives, blown-apart personalities and destroyed brain cells.

If Justin was an indirect victim — or, to the initiated, a hero — of the death cult of the late eighties and nineties, he was a direct victim of those forms of Rock that, since the mid-sixties, could be experienced in an enhanced form only through life-and-health-destroying drugs.

The *modus* of the fat cats behind the drug trade is, 'Get them on marijuana/cannabis first then it will be a cinch to heave them into heroin, LSD, ecstasy, whatever . . . .'

Marijuana/cannabis is a preparation from the dried flowering tops of the hemp plant and is smoked, chewed or drunk to induce euphoria. Slang equivalents include 'pot'; 'grass'; 'weed'; and, as a cigarette, 'joint' and 'reefer'. It is fashionable among politicians to talk about legalizing marijuana. 'After all,' said one, '250 million people of all economic and social classes, all ages and all races throughout the world are into it . . . .'

The ingredient in marijuana that produces the drug effect is *tetrahydrocannabinol* (THC), although smoking marijuana may release over 150 other compounds, most of which have potential physiological effects in the body. The amount of THC and other resins determines the potency ('grade') of marijuana. It is available to most 11-year-olds just outside — or sometimes inside — the playground of their schools.

Trendy politicians notwithstanding, not all trips are 'cool'; there are millions of accounts of 'bummers' even from this relatively soft drug. Even when there is no 'bummer', the THC has a long-term, as well as a short-term, effect upon the brain and, almost certainly, upon the chromosomes. Between 80 and 90 per cent of all heroin addicts use marijuana before becoming involved with narcotics.[6] Even those arguing for the legalization of marijuana agree that it cannot be categorized as 'harmless'. They base their arguments on scientific data that cigarettes are equally damaging to health, and that cigarettes are legal.

Heroin is a white, odourless, bitter, crystalline compound derived from morphine, and is a highly-addictive narcotic. By the mid-seventies it was as easy to 'cop' heroin as it was to get marijuana.[7] Because 4 milligrams of the drug injected intravenously have the same effect as 30 milligrams taken orally, hypodermics are frequently used. The alternative to 'shooting' is 'snorting'. A 'skin popper' injects the drug subcutaneously or into a muscle; while a 'main liner' injects it into a vein. 'Main lining' results in veins becoming swollen, blocked or 'collapsed'.

Physiologically, heroin sets off a myriad of reactions, ranging from nausea to respiratory depression, from decreased pain perception to a decrease in body temperature, from a general 'heavy' feeling in the limbs to swift changes in mood that sometimes result in extreme excitability. 'People who turn to heroin view their lives as a never-ending series of painful and traumatic experiences. Each heroin addict in his own particular way *seeks* to be narcotized out of perceiving the world around him . . . .'[8] Addiction sets in within a month. After a short time, the new heroin addicts need more and more of the drug to produce its euphoric effect. For the addicts, heroin is the overwhelming passion of their lives, though they typically feel 'cheated' as premature ageing sets in, along with liver infections, chronic skin ulcers and heart problems.

Cocaine/Crack. Cocaine hydrochloride is derived from the leaves of the Andean coca shrub, and the white powder is either sniffed or injected. Crack is the street name given to cocaine that has been purified and separated from its hydrochloride base. It can take the form of small white nuggets which are smoked and inhaled.

The history of cocaine is a long one. Coca leaves were chewed by the Incas hundreds of years ago. It was first marketed in Europe as a hay fever and sinusitis remedy. Freud advocated it as a stimulant, local anaesthetic, and treatment for syphilis and asthma.

Cocaine 'highs' produce a feeling of omnipotence and wellbeing. Protracted cocaine use produces paranoia and hallucinations. Repeated doses produce extreme agitation and anxiety. Excessive doses lead to death from respiratory depression, convulsions or heart rhythm disturbances.

Ecstasy (sometimes known as 'e' or 'disco biscuits'). Its active ingredient is a stimulant known as MDMA. First synthesized in 1912, it had no medical or commercial use. It came into popular use in the Raves of the late eighties.

An ecstasy 'high' takes the form of a euphoric rush or a feeling of serenity. It produces nausea, dry mouth and a rise in blood pressure when it is taken. High doses over a long period can produce anxiety, panic, confusion, insomnia and possibly psychosis. Fifty deaths in Britain have been directly traced to the drug in the last five years. Most of those who have died have exhibited symptoms connected with heatstroke. It is thought that the cumulative effects of MDMA (which as a stimulant makes it possible for the addict to dance for long periods without feeling exhausted) and dehydration from dancing in hot nightclubs have caused this. Some evidence suggests that ecstasy triggers the body's release of anti-diuretic hormones, which limit the effectiveness of the kidneys at processing fluids. Some people have responded to the stimulant aspect of the drug with very high blood pressure, causing heart attack or brain haemorrhage.

LSD. The origin and primary effects of LSD have already been examined. It is by far the most powerful of the hallucinogens. Oral doses as low as 20 micrograms may induce profound psychological and physiological effects. Acute LSD use can result in changes of mood and perception with visual illusions. Chronic use results in derangement of abstract thinking and memory, and can produce schizophrenic-form psychoses.[9] 'LSD does not *make* you psychotic. But it can and does bring certain mental disorders to the surface of your consciousness . . . .'[10] As a result, its effects include severe anxiety/panic attacks and psychotic-type reactions that result from garbage dredged from the sub-conscious. Case studies reveal a few instances of 'voices' — normally associated with schizophrenia — but Justin's direct, detailed instructions from his 'voices' would appear to be specific to his case.

It has been suggested that some 'garbage' had been 'dredged from his sub-conscious'.

Accepting that as a working hypothesis, what *could* the 'garbage' have been?

[1]*The Daily Mail*, 23 February 1996. [2]William Braden, *The Private Sea: LSD and the Search for God* (1967). [3]Steve Turner, *Hungry for Heaven: Rock and Roll and the Search for Redemption* (Hodder, 1994 edition), page 86. [4]Ibid. [5]Ibid, pages 87-89. [6]Mark Lieberman, *The Dope Book: All About Drugs*, page 83. [7]Ibid, page 113; *The Observer*, 1 October 1978. [8]Lieberman, op cit, page 123. [9]Harrison's *Principles of Internal Medicine*, 12th edition, 1991. [10]Lieberman, page 102; *Drugs Close to Home* (Review and Herald, 1987); *Drugs and Solvents* (European Drug Prevention Week, 1994); *Drugs: A Guide to the Uses and Abuses* (Supplement to *The Independent on Sunday*, 28 January 1996).

The Rise of the Occult

There has been an occult explosion in the last thirty years. It has partly come about as the result of the beliefs and lifestyles of Rock people, and the use they have made of occult/satanic imagery in their lyrics, videos, and album covers.

But the origins of the occult are far removed from popular culture.

The first modern manifestations of the occult. Authors cannot agree on exactly when and where the first modern manifestations of hard-core occult phenomena occurred.

To find out, we have to go to the occultists themselves.

The most detailed and authoritative account is found in Sir Arthur Conan Doyle's *The History of Spiritualism* (in two volumes; 1926). Conan Doyle, the creator of Sherlock the sleuth, was also a spiritist and a witness over many years to a wide variety of occult/paranormal phenomena.

Conan Doyle is up front about being an opponent of Christianity. To him, the rise of the occult — particularly in Spiritualism — was 'the most important development in the history of the world since the Christ episode . . . '.

'The father of our new knowledge of supernal matters', writes Conan Doyle, 'was Emanuel Swedenborg.' Swedenborg was a 'clairvoyant medium' whom Conan Doyle compares with Christ Himself.

Swedenborg (1699-1772) reacted violently against a Lutheran upbringing. Nevertheless, Conan Doyle believed that he was always handicapped by 'his tiresome exegesis of the Scriptures', however unorthodox that exegesis was.

Swedenborg was 55 when he had his first 'spiritual communication' with what Conan Doyle persistently terms 'The Other Side'. The philosopher Kant, a contemporary of Swedenborg, investigated and authenticated certain of his claims, including Swedenborg's vivid description while in Gothenburg of a fire that was taking place in Stockholm, 300 miles away. From the night of this fire — in Swedenborg's own words — 'the world of the spirits, hell and heaven, were open to me'. A system of deep breathing 'psychic exercises' was developed by Swedenborg, identical, says Conan Doyle, with 'the Indian system of Yoga'. But Swedenborg was primarily preoccupied with 'the other world to which we go after death'. And the 'New Church' which he founded, of which he was the prophet, was primarily preoccupied with endeavouring to contact those 'beyond the grave'.

Conan Doyle enrols Edward Irving (1792-1834) among the precursors of Spiritualism. Irving, though 'cramped by theology', says Conan Doyle, saw 'spiritual manifestations' from 1830 to 1833. The psychic phenomena evident in Irving's congregations involved 'strange tongues', and being rendered semi-conscious but in a kind of ecstasy. Conan Doyle deplores the fact that the 'charismatics' themselves, at length, began to attribute their tongues-speaking outbursts to 'a diabolical source'.[1]

'As the psychic cloud of other-world powers slowly settled upon the earth,' writes Conan Doyle, 'it found its real response among the Shakers of America.' In 1837, there were sixty groups of Shakers. At the time, the happenings in their meetings were closely-guarded secrets, their elders being concerned that they might be 'consigned to bedlam' if the truth came out. The phenomena were actually described in two books written well after the event.

The Shakers, apparently, invited the spirits to possess

them. This 'the invaders' were happy to do. Conan Doyle believed that 'the spirits' in question were dead red Indians, drawing this conclusion from the descriptions of the highly irregular behaviour in the closed Shaker meetings.[2]

Nevertheless, argues Conan Doyle, the real bridge between the early occult manifestations and the full flowering of the occult in modern Spiritualism was in the experience of Andrew Jackson Davis (1826-1910). A man without formal education, Davis, nevertheless, became 'a conduit pipe through which flowed the knowledge of the spirit world'. At first came clairaudience (hearing spirit voices); then came clairvoyance (communication with 'the other side'); then came out-of-body experiences.

Davis had, Conan Doyle argued, a wider experience with the spirit world because 'he was more or less untouched by conventional Christianity'.

The clapboard homestead in Hydesville. A vital date for the dawn of demonism was 31 March 1848.

Hydesville was a hamlet in upper New York State. The Fox family had moved into a clapboard dwelling there on 11 December 1847. The family included Kate, 11, and Margaret, 14.

The rappings began a few weeks after they had moved into the house. By mid-March, 1848, they were a source of irritation to the Foxes. 'Sometimes they were a mere knocking; at other times they sounded like the movement of furniture . . . .' At first the girls slept together for company and then, when the beds in the house began to shake, they moved into their parents' bedroom.

An extensive search was made of the property. There was no 'natural' explanation, it was concluded. The locals gossiped about a tinker who had met a violent death in the vicinity. On 31 March, Kate decided to throw out a challenge to the unseen world: 'Mr

Splitfoot, do as I do.' After what Conan Doyle considers were 'flippant' words, the Fox girls began to work out a sort of Morse code with the alien force inhabiting their home. Every snap of their fingers was echoed by a knock. 'The spiritual telegraph was working at last!' exults Conan Doyle.

The parents became involved. As the girls had done already, they, too, addressed a series of questions to the unseen world. They discovered that whatever entities were behind the knockings, they were party to information of which no human was aware. Needless to say, 'the spirits' confirmed the story of the tinker. On 11 April, a skeleton was discovered in a tin box (preserved to this day at the headquarters of the American Spiritualists).

Soon the clapboard homestead was receiving hundreds of visitors. Among the visitors was US Congressman Robert Dale Owen, eager to authenticate the 'old Splitfoot connection'.

But Mrs Fox, till that point a Methodist, was seriously disturbed by what was happening. Kate and Margaret were strangely attracted by the alien association.

Attempts were made to split them up. The two girls were sent to different relatives in different homes. But the occult phenomena followed them.

First in Upper New York State, then beyond, people were drawn into the Spiritualist movement. A theory — almost a theology — began to accumulate around it. Certain individuals, it was argued, had 'spirit magnetism'; such people were 'natural mediums'.

The Spiritualists began to proselytize. As early as 14 November 1849, they had hired the Corinthian Hall in Rochester. Rappings occurred on cue. Governor Tallmadge, who was also a US senator, began to take an interest. On two separate occasions and of two separate mediums he asked the question: 'What is the purpose of the new cult?' On both occasions the answer was: 'It is to draw mankind together in harmony and to convince sceptics of the immortality of the soul.'

The Fox family made a tour of the western states. Katie and Margaret gave regular seances, and seances became all the rage.

Despite the irregular behaviour of the Fox sisters from time to time and the exposure of some mediums as frauds, Spiritualism spread as few movements have. From the early 1870s it grew in England. Levitation, as well as rapping, 'spirit lights', 'direct writing' and the appearance of 'materialized hands', became part of the Spiritualist repertoire.

According to Conan Doyle's own testimony, the effect of the paranormal phenomena, and of their fame, on the Fox sisters was disastrous. Within twenty-five years of the 1848 date, both women were 'seriously unbalanced' alcoholics, with a police record for violence to their children. Both Kate and Margaret had, says Conan Doyle, 'a sordid end' in the early 1890s; 'Their end was one of sadness and gloom.' Elsewhere, a disproportionate number of Spiritualists ended their days in psychiatric hospitals.

But the movement had taken off. And by the 1890s the literati of America and Europe were involved in it. For some it was a fad and a fashion; for others it mattered more to them than anything else. The talk everywhere was of 'communion with departed friends and relations'. There are scores of authenticated accounts of 'voices from the dead' speaking through trance mediums.

Among the luminaries of the Spiritualist movement was Professor William Crookes (1832-1919), a Fellow of the Royal Society, knighted by Queen Victoria in 1897 and given the Order of Merit in 1910. Crookes had begun by attempting to 'expose Spiritualism', but had ended in being taken over by it. In the *Journal of Science*, at various times, Crookes described materialized figures 'built up from the ectoplasm of the medium' that manifested themselves in seances. His experience of 'direct voice phenomena' was that, at first, the medium spoke in her own voice, but eventually it either divided into two voices or took on the accent of the assumed dead individual. Crookes claimed to possess forty-four photographs, of varying quality, of spirit phenomena, including one of his own personal 'familiar'.

Spiritualism at its height. In the 1860s the Court of France — under Napoleon III and the colourful Empress Eugenie — boasted levitation and pianos that played themselves as a regular attraction at dinner parties.

In Russia the occult had an influence on the intellectuals, the boyars (aristocracy), and over the house of Romanov. Indeed, the influence of the medium Rasputin, and the disastrous consequences of the advice he gave to the Tsar heading the Russian armies at the Eastern Front in World War I, played a major role in bringing down the Royal House of Russia.

In the twenty years that straddled the turn of the century, it was exceptional to find a British literary figure who was not, at some stage, caught up in Spiritualism. The prospect of 'communicating with the dear departed' was intriguing.

In the course of World War I, Spiritualists took advantage of the uncertainty felt by wives and mothers with regard to their men at the western front. On a number of celebrated instances, however, after their lost loved ones had been seen and heard at seances, the 'deceased' arrived home safe and well!

There were also many examples of the lives of mediums, including the most famous English medium

Charles Foster, being made miserable or horrific through the behaviour of the unseen 'spirits'.

But Sir Arthur Conan Doyle never doubted the importance, the authenticity, and the supernatural phenomena that accompanied Spiritualism. The second volume of his *History* is taken up with the defence of Spiritualism against scientists and Christians who attacked it. As far as he was concerned, 'the unseen wall' had been breached. And, from beyond the grave, the voices of the dead were being heard through the throats of mediums, and the forms of the dead were being manifested through the ectoplasm that came out of the 'bodily orifices' of the mediums.

That trickery was used by some charlatans is beyond dispute. Equally beyond dispute is that much of the hard-core occult activity surrounding Spiritualism was beyond scientific explanation. That is not to say, of course, that the phenomena had any connection with the spirits of the dead. They did not. An explanation of Spiritualism and the phenomena that accompanied its growth must wait for a later chapter.

At this point it is important to note that, by the end of World War I, it was becoming evident that another, even more sinister, movement had developed. It was a movement that had paralleled the growth of Spiritualism from the start but had lived in its shadow. Whereas Spiritualism claimed to have established contact with dead relations and friends — a contact that generally resulted in, at best, a meaningless message — the other movement claimed to 'channel' the spirits of long-dead 'gurus', 'masters' and 'christs' from past millennia. Further, it claimed that in the utterances of these 'masters' was a 'wisdom of the ages' that would ultimately remove and supplant Christianity.

This second, more sinister, occult movement began,

not in Hydesville, USA, but in a tiny hamlet in southern Russia. Its founder was the daughter of an aristocrat.[3]

All this may seem a million miles away from Justin's suicide. In fact, the connection is a strong one. The role of the paranormal in those final weeks is one that cannot be ignored.

[1]Sir Arthur Conan Doyle, *The History of Spiritualism* (1926), volume 1, pages 17-29. [2]Ibid, pages 30-36. [3]Peter Washington, *Theosophy and the Emergence of the Western Guru* (Secker, 1993).

Note. On spirit-possession and mediumship, see David Burnett, *Unearthly Powers* (March, 1988), pages 114-139, 163-197.

New Age and the Occult

Origins. Helena Petrovena Blavatsky was the daughter of a minor Russian aristocrat. As a teenager she was weird and wilful, marrying the elderly General Blavatsky at 17. The relationship lasted barely three months and Madame Blavatsky began her wanderings from country to country. These wanderings took her to Egypt, Tibet and India. At various times she was a circus performer, a concert pianist and a popular spiritist medium. A 'shaman' she met in Tibet directed her further into the occult. On a brief visit to St Petersburg, she dazzled society with demonstrations of her psychic powers.

From Tibet she went to India and settled in an ashram, a commune presided over by a guru. In the ashram she learned what she later called 'the wisdom of the East'.

- She learned transcendental meditation (TM), mental relaxation promoted by the repeated utterance of a mantra. The point of meditation was to 'empty the mind'. TM was the essential preparation for many Hindu spiritual exercises, including 'channelling'.

- Blavatsky claimed that 'channelling' put her in touch with 'the Beyond', the 'Great Brotherhood of the Masters'. Trance-channelling was almost indistinguishable from seance-mediumship which Blavatsky had practised for years. However, she believed that the difference was vital. Whereas mediumship had been a hit-and-miss affair, intended to make contact with deceased relatives and friends, trance-channelling was intended to contact 'the masters' who had, Blavatsky believed, included Buddha, Plato and Franz Anton Mesmer. Madame Blavatsky believed that by channelling the 'enlightened ones' of lost civilizations she could, through their 'wisdom', redirect the world to a 'new age' through a new belief system.

• Blavatsky also absorbed the key beliefs of both Buddhism and Hinduism. These beliefs included reincarnation — the idea that, through the 'wheel of Samsara', there was an endless round of lifetimes, the next 'life form' being dependent upon one's *karma*.

By 1874 Madame Blavatsky had migrated to the USA where, with Colonel H. S. Olcott (1832-1907), she founded the Theosophical Society in New York in 1875. Her home was, apparently, infested with 'spirits'. Visitors reported moving furniture, chandeliers that shook, unaccountable rappings and bangings, and the appearance of 'ghosts'. In 1877 she produced a series of books under the title *Isis Unveiled* which she claimed to have been 'spirit-written' (in fact, her handwriting was unintelligible!). In her 'occult room', she retired to practise channelling; to commune with the 'Mahatmas', the masters; and to write down their teachings and advice so that she might pass them on to the faithful.

By the time of her death in the spring of 1891, Madame Blavatsky was living in England. Here, as in America, she found a large following for her teachings. Many among the intelligentsia who looked down upon Spiritualism as tainted by charlatans and lower-class behaviour regarded membership of the Theosophical Society as *chic*.[1]

Following Blavatsky's death, Annie Besant — better known as a crusading atheist and campaigner for birth control — took over the leadership of the movement. Among those involved in the movement in the early decades of the twentieth century were W. B. Yeats, Aldous Huxley and G. B. Shaw. To the mix of Eastern religion and the hard-core occult, astrology was added during this period. Alice Bailey, the successor to Annie Besant, claimed to be the channeller of the 'master' Djwhal Khul. She claimed him as the real author of the shelfful of 'spirit-written' books produced during her lifetime. In 1949, Benjamin Creme succeeded her. Another channeller of Djwhal Khul, he, too, produced 'spirit-written' material.[2]

The Sixties. The so-called 'spirit-written' books of Madame Blavatsky and Alice Bailey had an essentially esoteric appeal. Until the 1960s, no one would have believed that the obscure concepts they contained would one day form the substance for a world-wide movement. Blavatsky's Theosophical Society had never numbered more than 100,000 members. In the mid-1990s, the New Age movement overspreads the planet like a foul miasma, numbering millions among its followers, including Hollywood's *glitterati*.[3]

The sixties made the difference.

When the Beatles returned from their excursion to India they brought with them not just LSD, but the basis of a whole new counter culture.

The Beatles had learned the beliefs that brought about their 'conversion' at the feet of the guru Maharishi Mahesh Yogi. Dressed in flowing white, his long greying beard tangled with the crystal beads round his neck, the image of the Maharishi was soon plastered on billboards all over the West. He emerged as a cult figure of the new era, epitomizing 'flower power', a father figure of the hippy generation.

What the Beatles had learned at the Maharishi's ashram at Rishikesh on the banks of the Ganges transformed their lyrics and gave them a crusade. Out went the 'She-loves-you-yea-yea-yea' lyrics; in came the texts, jargon and beliefs of the East. The mindless had given way to the esoteric. At a time when they topped the charts in every Western nation, without dispute the most popular singing group on the planet, Beatles George Harrison and John Lennon were working the esoteric East into the lyrics of their multi-million-selling records.[4]

Suddenly, the vocabulary of Hinduism and Buddhism was 'in'; reincarnation, yoga, meditation, TM and the rest.

If, as Nina Easton wrote in *The Los Angeles Times* magazine, Blavatsky might be called 'a god mother of the New Age movement', the Beatles were unquestionably its midwives.

New Age pacesetter Marilyn Ferguson still believed in the early seventies that the new mix of Eastern religion, astrology and hard-core occult was a movement without a name. However, years before, Alice Bailey had coined the phrase 'New Age'. By 1977 it would be accepted in the media as the name for the new movement.

The Seventies. Blavatsky, Annie Besant and their successors had trumpeted the channelled 'prophecies' and 'wisdom' of their hierarchy of 'ascended masters'. They had also paved the way for transcendental meditation, Zen, Hare Krishna, yoga, reincarnation, swamis, yogis and gurus — all of which were indispensable to the Beatles-inspired counter-culture, 'the youthquake' of the early seventies. Whether they understood its meaning or not, everyone was singing the title song of the musical *Hair*, 'It is the dawning of the age of Aquarius . . . .' The Age of Pisces was past, said Marilyn Ferguson in *The Aquarian Conspiracy*, and the Age of Aquarius was dawning; Christianity was on the out and would be replaced by the end of the century with the neo-pagan culture-religion of New Age.

In the early seventies, Indian gurus were flying West on one-way tickets — to become fabulously wealthy, especially in the USA. At the height of his popularity,

Bhagwan Shree Rajneesh induced 20,000 people a year to follow him in India, and 4,500 to live at his ashram in Oregon. He had ninety-three Rolls-Royces and a private army equipped with assault rifles and riot guns. Eighty-three per cent of his American followers were college educated.[5]

Anyone who was anyone among the *glitterati* practised TM. There were yogas for all occasions; mantra yoga, sidhi yoga, tantra yoga. Astrology became the biggest growth industry. Next in line was the 'human potential movement', spearheaded by 'humanistic' therapists of various mystical inclinations. New Age was soon offering a variety of 'alternative routes' to both physical and mental health. What had begun with acid dreams and Eastern gurus came to affect many areas of life.

The American-based gurus were preaching a pagan-religious ecstasy and, through mind-control techniques, introducing it to their myriad followers. Some saw a parallel between this and the 'ecstatic' movement affecting the Christian Church, but they were soon shouted down and shoved out on to the margins . . . .[6]

Will Baron was especially concerned with the impact of New Age ideas and practices upon the Christian Church. Most who have written about the New Age movement have done so from either an insider's or a Christian perspective. Will Baron's *Deceived by the New Age* (Pacific Press, 1990) is the authoritative narrative of Will's spiritual odyssey into, through and beyond New Age — back to Christianity. Will Baron lays bare the various *faces* — many innocuous, some even helpful — and *phases* of the New Age movement.

Will told me that his involvement began at a New Age health clinic in London, continued with a New Age brand of psychotherapy in Donegal — and ended with Will as a New Age 'channeller' in LA. He became a channeller of — no less! — Djwhal Khul, the 'ascended master' who normally favoured only the leaders of the movement. Alien voices spoke through Will, and images manifested themselves before him that would have more than impressed — indeed, astonished and terrified — a nineteenth-century spiritist.

But Will was given the specific task of infiltrating Christianity on behalf of the New Age movement, and was dispatched to the New Age training centre at Findhorn in Scotland to receive his necessary preparation. Will was trained in the Swedenborg method of expounding Scripture so as to con Christians. Instead of Djwhal Khul, he began to channel a new and horrific 'master' called 'Jesus Christ'.

In his infiltration of Christianity, however, Will was exposed, eventually, to the Gospel of the real Jesus Christ. His life was transformed and he was born again. Will believed that he had found in Scripture an exposé of New Age and had discovered that there was nothing 'new' about it.

The Eighties. By the end of the seventies an army of 'headliners' and 'honchos' were into New Age. The mass circulation *New Age Journal* and Mark Satin's book *New Age Politics* swept it into vogue. Marilyn Ferguson's *Aquarian Conspiracy* became its bible and agenda. Shirley Maclaine, with her prodigious output of books and New Age TV series (in addition to films), became its high priestess. *Time* magazine called her 'the New Agers' reigning whirling dervish'.

By the early eighties, Benjamin Creme, based in Britain, was reiterating the belief that by the end of the millennium the Age of Pisces (Christianity) would have been decisively replaced by the Age of Aquarius (New Age), but had added that the new age would be accompanied by a 'new world messiah', and a 'new world order'.

It was in the eighties that New Age became a truly mass movement. It took the radical materialism of that decade — Thatcherism, Reaganism, Milton Friedmanism — to provide New Age with a following of millions, including a disproportionate number of Hollywood and media *glitterati*. The yuppie culture proved an inadequate diet for the human spirit — and millions reacted against it. At the same time as, in the East, Communism was collapsing and there was a reaction towards Christianity, in the West it was becoming chic to be spiritual — but Western spirituality was taking on a pagan, New Age form.

New Age was all over the place. And not all of the places where it was found were bad places. It had become a 'designer religion', borrowing ideas from a whole range of world views and manifesting itself in the most trendy of quarters. To the Green movement it introduced a sort of neo-pantheism. New Agers rushed into various areas of alternative medicine, especially those based on Eastern, mystical ideas.

C. S. Lewis had once said that the real threat to Christianity came from Hinduism; and suddenly his throw-away line achieved a striking reality. On university campuses reincarnation was more widely believed, according to opinion polls, than the resurrection, and reincarnation disposes of sin and judgement by offering a whole series of lifetimes to work off a negative *karma*. No one mentioned that there was no forgiveness in Hinduism, and that the wheel of Samsara ground on, and ground down its adherents, India itself providing a less than ideal example of a Hindu utopia. Hindu and Buddhist meditation techniques were everywhere; and even Christian preachers could, here and there, be heard advocating meditation and 'visualization' techniques.

The Buddhist abandonment of God in pursuit of the 'god within' appealed to an amoral society, seeking justification for amoral behaviour.

The Nineties. By the end of the eighties so many had jumped on the New Age bandwagon, but not everyone appreciated the company. The term 'New Age' had become pejorative and some were trying to shake it off. In Britain, one-time soccer player and TV reporter David Icke, having become the chief spokesman for the Green Party, suddenly announced on TV that he was Jesus Christ. He later produced two books — inevitably 'spirit-written' — in which he explained the standard doctrine that there were many 'christs' of which he just happened to be one. But the damage had been done, and the British Green Party has never quite recovered its credibility.[7]

In the mid-nineties every shopping precinct has its specialist New Age shop full of books and crystals and other assorted paraphernalia. Retired Archbishop Robert Runcie told his biographer Humphrey Carpenter that Charles, Prince of Wales, had abandoned the Church by the early 1980s and 'was deeply into the Laurens van der Post spirituality'. Newspapers reviewing Runcie's biography called van der Post 'Charles's Western guru'. In his many books van der Post presented the complete New Age menu. In his *Times* obituary, 17 December 1996, he was quoted as saying that it was in the war years that he had discovered 'another person' within himself and begun to be directed by the 'other voice'. Diana, Princess of Wales, and Sarah, Duchess of York, reportedly on a regular basis, have sought the advice of tarot card readers and astrologers. Russia's best-known psychic was discovered to have been part of President

Yeltsin's inner circle of advisers.[8] The brightest stars in Hollywood's firmament — backers and producers, as well as actors and actresses — continue to be New Agers, some of them signed-up Scientologists. George Lucas and Steven Spielberg have produced valuable, as well as New Age-tarnished, work. Some of the New Age actors/actresses — John Travolta, Tom Cruise, Nicole Kidman and Sharon Gless — more often than not appear in big-screen productions, devoid of anything remotely New Age. But other adherents — Demi Moore, Mimi Rogers, and Sharon Stone — have an affinity for the sordid end of the market in which sex, ghouls, ghosties and peddled paranormal are standard fodder.[9]

But the big screen is not the only force influencing malleable minds. New Age is in the educational system, in work-training methods, and, according to some, even in church! But the darkest New Age penumbra covers Rock. To see how this came about, not for the first time we need to go back to the Beatles.

---

[1]Peter Washington, *Theosophy and the Rise of the Western Guru* (Secker, 1993); Ronald Enroth, *Lure of the Cults and New Religions* (IVP, 1987); *The Sunday Times*, 25 April 1993; *The Sunday Times: Books*, 9 June 1996. [2]Peter Washington, op cit; David Marshall, *The Devil Hides Out* (Autumn House, 1991); Brooks Alexander, 'The New Age Movement is Nothing New', *Eternity Magazine* (February 1988). [3]David Marshall, *New Age Versus the Gospel* (Autumn House 1993). [4]Michael Medved, 'The Corruption of Rock', *The Sunday Times*, 28 February 1993; *The Mail on Sunday*, 13 October 1996, page 25; Steve Turner, *Hungry for Heaven* (Hodder, 1994 edition), pages 46-56; *Time*, 29 February 1988. [5]Anthony Storr, *Feet of Clay: A Study of Gurus* (Harper Collins, 1996). [6]Ibid; Simon Jenkins, 'Under the Influence', *The Sunday Times: Books*, 9 June 1996. [7]*The Sunday Times*, 30 August 1992, News Review, page 5; Marilyn Ferguson, *Aquarian Conspiracy: Social Transformation in the 80s* (Tarcher, 1980). See the author's *New Age Versus the Gospel* (Autumn House, 1993), page 63. [8]Editorial; Stuart Wavell on Laurens van der Post; and Sophia Wells, 'Profit of Doom', *The Sunday Times*, Sections 3, 7 and 9, 6 October 1996; *The Times* 17 December 1996, page 17; Andrew Brown, *Independent on Sunday*, 8 September 1996; Stuart Wavell in *The*

Sunday Times, 25 August 1996; Humphrey Carpenter, *Robert Runcie, The Reluctant Archbishop* (Hodder, 1996), page 221; 'Yeltsin and the Occult', *The Sunday Times*, 12 February 1995; *The Times*, 15 May 1995. See *The Independent on Sunday*, 31 December 1995; *The Guardian*, 17 December 1996, pages 3 and 15. ⁹*The Sunday Times*, 15 September 1996; *Sunday Express*, 19 June 1993, pages 48, 49. See Bob and Gretchen Passantino, *When the Devil Dares Your Kids* (Eagle, 1996), pages 105-129; David Marshall, op cit, pages 78-80; David Marshall, 'The New Age is not so new after all', *Dialogue: College and University*, volume 7, number 3, pages 5-7; Anthony Storr, op cit; Mark Bubeck, *The Satanic Revival* (Scripture Press, 1991), pages 26, 27.

Rock, the Satanic Connection

New Age, the neo-pagan movement that threatens to replace Christianity, is not a 'movement' in the sense that a trade union or a political party is. With the single exception of that hard New Age nugget Scientology, New Agers do not 'sign up' or hold membership.

It may appear ridiculous. . . . The claims made by Benjamin Creme in 1996 that the New Age messiah, 'the Lord Maitreya', was in the wings, waiting to assume his world role, gave many the impression that there was a New Age conspiracy to take over the planet. Conspiracy theorists soon fleshed out the idea and, in their writings, nominated assorted gurus, professors, Hollywood moguls and miscellaneous fat cats as members of 'a New Age hierarchy', prime movers in the world-domination conspiracy. In doing this, of course, they totally misunderstood the character of the movement. It is all pervasive in its influence, but has almost as many faces as it has adherents.

Many of those appearing on the media to represent New Age seem more than slightly ridiculous. As Michael Pye wrote, 'Nine in the morning, New York time, you can turn on the TV and contemplate mediums, witches, people who have been stolen by spaceships, people who have gone out of their bodies — a printing company executive who went "through the ceiling into the astral", a witch who wants her son's respect, a line-up with only the irrational in common . . . .'[1]

Bombarded by miracles, 'X-Files', prime-time specials about angels, with a whole millennial parade of weird notions — the average US viewer might be tempted to laugh off the whole thing. TV has bred its own post-modernism: fact, fiction, the canonical and the popular — no longer categories or definitions, just time slots. The psychic prophet, the terrorism expert, the Secretary of State for Industry, Roseanne, X-Files (or similar), all follow one another with equal weight.

On comes a Harvard professor to argue that 'reality is layered, that UFO stories are so similar they must be true'. He is followed by a succession of chat-show psychics, all given a respectful audience. They make predictions, unembarrassed that, in turn, they had prophesied that Castro would be assassinated in 1992, that Princess Diana would pose nude for *Playboy* in 1994 and that Whoopi Goldberg would enter a convent in 1996! There are innumerable stories — also on chat shows — of those who have been 'abducted' for varying lengths of time by UFOs. With a media diet like that, who can blame the many-headed multitude for being a touch sardonic, not to say sceptical?

The totally sceptical and the totally credulous are in almost equal danger.

Satanism and suicide. Since the eighteenth century there has been a movement to make contact with 'the spirits' and, in the last twenty years, it has become a mass movement. Under the dark penumbra on its outer perimeter, there have been black deeds. Parallel with the rise of the new paganism has been the rise of a new witchcraft craze and a greater following than at any pre-vious time for overt Satanism.[2] This becomes apparent only when a symptom of the new craze makes it into the media.

In both the US and the UK, since the early eighties, the increased popularity of witchcraft has led to a massive increase in the incidence of the ritual, sexual abuse of children.[3]

Satanism hits the headlines when it leads to crime or to suicide.

In February 1996, Ruth Fleming, 22, Jane Greenhow, 23, and Stephen Bateman, 22, committed suicide. They died within twenty-four hours of one another, but a thousand miles apart. The triple suicide was investigated by a team of London journalists[4] and by our own researcher, Vivienne James, to whom the Bateman family was well known. Vivienne found that the three suiciders were all involved in Death Metal music and that they had formed part of a larger group that gathered regularly to read their Satanic bibles. Prior to the triple suicide, other members of the group, terror-struck, had disappeared for lengthy periods.

Behind the triple suicide, it appeared, was a pact. The suicides were carried out at the end of a seven-week trek, of criss-crossing the USA in rented cars and staying in cheap hotels. Fleming and Bateman shot themselves with hired pistols; Greenhow was found in a hire car on a forest trail in California.

The investigation traced the three back to a Rave session at a house in Andover, Hampshire. The clues left behind included the suicide note, Rave music tapes, and tapes of far Right (Nazi) groups singing songs like 'The Dance of Death', 'Suffering', and 'Battle Grin'. The neo-Nazis apparently believe that, beyond death, they will arrive in Valhalla, a mythical hall of slain warriors.

Greenhow and Fleming had collected first-class honours degrees in Physics from Leicester University in 1994.

The Times investigation turned up evidence that an enthusiasm for Death Metal music had led to an absorption with the 'more sinister sound', Rave. Bateman had, it appeared, discovered the music of 'Aryan White

Supremacy, an international network of music distribution companies linked by the Internet that act as a front for extremist violence'[4]. There was both a Satanic and a Nazi connection.

Satanism: An insider's view. In the early nineties, Audrey Harper came out of witchcraft to embrace Christianity — and lived to publish her story. More recently, Miss Harper has published *Deliverance Means Love*, in which she provides a valuable insight into the relationship between witchcraft, Satanism, demonology — and Heavy Metal music. While involved in witchcraft she came under a great deal of pressure to listen to Heavy Metal. 'Listen to the words,' she was repeatedly urged. She writes, 'As I put the earphones to my ears the noise hit me, and I screwed my face up in agony. After what seemed like ten minutes, but was in fact two seconds, I ripped the earphones off and admitted defeat. If I was to get hold of the words, I would have to try some other way.' Eventually the words — a lyric from a song by Slayer — were actually written down for her:

> *Candles glowing, altars burn:*
> *Virgin's death is needed there.*
> *Sacrifice to Lucifer,*
> *My master.*
> *Bring the chalice,*
> *Raise the knife,*
> *Welcome to my sacrifice.*
> *Plunge the dagger in*
> *Her breast;*
> *SACRIFICE.*
> *Demons rejoice:*
> *Sacrifice,*
> *Sacrifice.*

Harper comments: 'This is a description of a real ritual in a Satanic temple. It doesn't matter whether the group are devil worshippers or not — they are still promoting Satanism, and it's sick.'[5]

Following her escape from witchcraft and Satanism, Harper went on record with regard to her deep concern at the number of youth in 'normal society', who spend their lives with Walkmans plugged in, listening to Heavy Metal music with lyrics of the sort she had encountered in Satanism. She insists that the lyrics promote death.

Harper emphasizes that implicit in the lyrics is the occult promise: Death means freedom. She continues: 'Newspaper reports revealed that at least two young people have committed suicide as a result of listening to this particular song and ten more have signed a suicide pact. We don't find life by looking at death. . . . So many have been drawn into something which seemed harmless, but which proved to lead to bondage and fear.'

Satanism and Rock. The occult and nihilistic content of Rock was introduced at the same time as drugs and New Age. In other words, following the Beatles' return from India in 1965.

Early Rock stars such as Elvis Presley, Little Richard and Buddy Holly had emerged from Christian backgrounds and found their music in conflict with Christianity.[6] After 1965, the Rock scene developed a strong anti-Christian edge. In 1965, Paul McCartney announced: 'None of us believes in God.' At times John Lennon was brutally blasphemous. Clergy, the disabled, and Jesus Christ were the targets of his most cruel barbs. Beatles' press officer Derek Taylor announced: 'It's incredible! Here are four boys from Liverpool. They're rude, they're profane, they're vulgar, and they've taken over the world. It's as if they'd founded a new religion. They're completely anti-Christ. I mean, I'm anti-Christ as well, but they're so anti-Christ they shock *me*, which isn't an easy thing.'

It soon became evident that the anti-Christ crusade was actually New Age. As if quoting from a New Age textbook, McCartney announced: 'God is a force we are all a part of.' George Harrison added: 'It's as though someone suddenly wipes away all you're taught or brought up to believe as a child and says, "That's not it".'

'We're all one,' Harrison announced in 1967. 'It's a good vibration which makes you feel good. These vibrations that you get through Yoga, cosmic chants and things like that, I mean it's such a buzz . . . .' McCartney bubbled: 'The great thing about people like Babaji and Christ, and all the governors who have transcended, is that they've got out of the reincarnation cycle. They've reached the bit where they're just there. They don't have to zoom back. They're planning the spiritual thing for us.'

At one stage Donovan, the Rolling Stones, and the Beach Boys, as well as the Beatles, were under the spell of the Maharishi Mahesh Yogi, the 55-year-old guru founder of the Spiritual Regeneration Movement.[7]

Historian of Rock, Steve Turner, has written: 'Pop people who had turned their backs on Christianity without a second thought swallowed the utterances of the gurus wholesale. Through chanting you could get "blissed out".' In Hindu teaching, they knew, music was one of the paths to god-consciousness. It released souls trapped in the world of delusion and was a divine art, dignified by the gods Krishna, Brahma and Shiba.

The Who, who favoured Sai Baba,[8] attempted to use their music as an allegorical description of a journey from spiritual darkness to 'god-realization'.

Then, in the early seventies, came disillusionment. . . . The gurus turned out to be rather less than 'god men' when evidence emerged of their fabulous wealth, their Swiss bank accounts, the number of Rolls-Royces they owned and how they abused women.

Going to the devil. Perhaps it was this disillusionment that led to the obsession with Satanism. Perhaps the Satanic obsession was just the hardcore occult element in New Age.

Steve Turner writes, 'Like no Rock group before them the Rolling Stones invoked the devil, entitling an album Their Satanic Majesty's Request. They even took on the persona of Lucifer and, on many occasions, played on occult association.' On a TV special Jagger ripped off his black shirt to reveal a tattoo of the devil on his chest.[9]

Some saw it as all part of a commercial image, an invention of an early-date Saatchi and Saatchi similar. But, in fact, for Jagger it was the beginning of a fascination with occult literature. Rolling Stone Keith Richards was quite open about the 'Satan trip', and his involvement with magic rituals and witchcraft. Anita Pallenberg, at different times girlfriend to Keith Richards and Brian Jones, states that inevitably the 'Satan trip' influenced their lyrics — as well as their nightmares. Jones, she said, was 'a haunted man'.

Christian analysts caught on to the diabolic content of Rock early in the seventies. Unfortunately, however, they went off at a tangent, looking for evidence of 'back-masking' (never very convincing). The lyrics played forwards were significant enough!

In the album, The Damned Patti Smith, in a band titled 'Gloria', sang, 'Jesus died for somebody's sins — but not mine!' Ridiculing Jesus became one of the more-or-less constant themes in Rock lyrics during this period. Nina Hagan habitually mixed the sacred, the profane and the blasphemous in her lyrics. John Lennon was rather more than recording his indifference to God in his song 'Imagine'. There can be little doubt that he meant it when he said, 'Christianity will vanish and shrink. Jesus will go.'

The group Ludichrist echoed Lennon's sentiments in many lyrics, notably in the album 'Immaculate Deception'.

Eric Holmberg analysed the content of Anton LaVey's *The Satanic Bible*.[10] LaVey, founder of the Church of Satan, has acted as consultant for many Hollywood movies involved with the occult. In a verse-by-verse examination of *The Satanic Bible*, Holmberg discovered a plethora of direct parallels with Rock lyrics, videos and album covers, over a period between 1971 and 91. The actual litany of Satan from *The Satanic Bible* was reproduced in lyrics in the album Diamanda Galas.

By no means a fundamentalist fanatic, Holmberg clearly came to view Rock music as little more than a vehicle for the advancement of anti-Christian/Satanic ideas. While Holmberg spent a disproportionate time in analysis of the fringes of Rock, the case he made is one that must be taken seriously.

It is not unreasonable, then, to see the Rock industry as it entered the eighties as a vital ingredient of the counter culture aimed to undermine, perhaps destroy, Christianity.

Dr David Elkind, in his authoritative work *The Hurried Child*, expounds the view that the most underestimated influence on youth is the music industry.

An issue of the *US National Review* on the Rock industry kicked off with: 'Rock's sheer pervasiveness makes it the most profound value-shaper in existence today. Unless you are deaf, it's virtually guaranteed that Rock music has affected your view of the world.'

'Never before has destructive occultism been hawked so crassly directly to teenagers through metal music, movies and videos, books, and even comic books and magazines,' wrote Bob and Gretchen Passantino. 'Today's teenagers are confronted on every side with the commercialized occult. Their favourite bands recite Satanic lyrics; T-shirts are emblazoned with Satanic pentacles; top grossing movies feature immortal Satanic murderers; comic super heroes call on demonic powers to vanquish the enemy; and the most popular mail order jewellery involves inverted cross earrings, human skull charm bracelets, and goat's head necklaces.'[11]

In the light of the accepted influence of Rock, it was almost chilling to read in *The Hit Parader* (1985) the words of Angus Young of AC/DC: 'Someone else is steering me . . . I become possessed when I'm on stage . . . .'

'Possessed' — by what? By whom?

[1]*The Scotsman*, 29 May 1995; *The Sunday Review* in *The Independent on Sunday*, 5 January 1997. [2]M. I. Bubeck, *The Satanic Revival* (Scripture Press, 1992); Kevin Logan, *Satanism and the Occult* (Kingsway, 1994); David Marshall, *The Devil Hides Out* (Autumn House, 1991). [3]Kevin Logan, *Satanism and the Occult* (Kingsway, 1994), pages 34-60; *The Observer*, 16 September 1990, 10 March 1991, 17 March 1991; Dianne Core, *Chasing Satan* (Gunter Books, 1991); Pat Pulling, *The Devil's Web: Who is Stalking Your Children?* (Word, 1990), pages 65-76; Beatrix Campbell, 'Vortex of Evil', *Social Work Today*, 5 October 1990; Bob Passantino, *Occult Crime* (Eagle, 1996), pages 131-160; Mark Bubeck, *The Satanic Revival* (Scripture Press, 1991), pages 14-18; Tim Lenton, 'Ritual Child Abuse', *Christian Weekly News*, 15 March 1991; J. G. Friesen, *Multiple Personality Disorders* (Here's Life Publishers, 1991). [4]*The Sunday Times*, 25 February 1996. [5]Audrey Harper, *Deliverance Means Love* (Kingsway, 1995), pages 46-49. [6]Steve Turner, *Hungry For Heaven: Rock and Roll and the Search for Redemption* (Hodder, 1994 edit), pages 12-20. [7]Andre Nataf, *Dictionary of the Occult* (Wordsworth, 1994). [8]Margaret Nichole, *Psychics and Mystics* (Hamlyn, 1994), pages 97-99. [9]Steve Turner, op cit, pages 81 *et seq.* [10]*Hell's Bells: The Dangers of Rock and Roll* (Reel to Real Videos). [11]Bob and Gretchen Passantino, *When the Devil Dares Your Kids* (Eagle, 1996), pages 107, 108.

Techno Paganism

Distinguishing between Rock groups/performers who were Satanist by conviction, and those advised to adopt the trappings in order to project a market-grabbing image was difficult in the eighties. But while, at one stage, it was argued that the former led popular taste, while the latter followed it, it soon became apparent that both were fulfilling the same function.

The radical materialism of the eighties was an inadequate diet for the human spirit. The old established churches did not appeal and failed to make an impact. Youth turned towards pagan spirituality. Those alienated from an establishment content to preside over an underclass, a large proportion of whose youth had no prospect of permanent employment, aimed to find the most shocking means to rebel: a flirtation with Satan.

The Satanic side of New Age. Aleister Crowley (1875-1947) was, arguably, 'Madame Blavatsky's most horrid offspring' (G. B. Shaw).

Crowley was drawn into the occult while still at Cambridge. But it was for his views on eroticism that he first attracted public attention. Bisexual, Crowley had scandalous affairs with public figures, male and female. Along with W. B. Yeats, poet, and Bram Stoker, author of *Dracula*, Crowley founded the Order of the Golden Dawn. According to *The Dictionary of the Occult*, as grand master of this order, Crowley formed a homosexual partnership with a well-known novelist. 'The two of them abandoned themselves to magic, and Crowley declared his wish to become a "saint of Satan" and to be known as the "Great Beast" and "The wickedest man alive".'[1]

Crowley authored *Magic in Theory and Practice* and

delighted to dress up as a priest, performing black masses and 'mystical marriages'.

The Order of the Golden Dawn was noted for extreme practices but, in 1900, Crowley was expelled from it — *for extreme practices!* He chose to travel the world, becoming a Buddhist monk and being initiated into Tantrism while in India. In Paris he associated with Rodin, Rilke, Somerset Maugham and Rose Edith Kelley, his 'scarlet woman' whom he was to marry. It was in Cairo that a spiritist medium in a trance revealed to Crowley the 'ultimate mystery', that led him to found the Order of the Silver Star.

Soon, with others, he was journeying into the Algerian desert to meet with Ultimate Evil. He was later found half dead with exhaustion. His subsequent exploits involved addiction to heroin, a wildly promiscuous lifestyle, and behaviour based on the belief that he was a vampire.

Few who knew Crowley argued with the assertion that he was demon-possessed.

First Hendrix then Bowie. . . . In the late 1970s David Bowie became utterly fascinated with the life and writings of Aleister Crowley. The members of Led Zeppelin became so obsessed with Crowley's beliefs and writings that it is fairly widely accepted that they engaged in certain of the rituals he recommended, involving the slaughter of animals. Their guitarist, Jimmy Page, hired Satanist Charles Pace to paint murals.[2]

Crowley's *Magic in Theory and Practice* became required reading in Hard Rock circles at the beginning of the eighties. The record labels of Led Zeppelin quoted, approvingly, Crowley's dictum: 'There is no law but ''Do what thou wilt''.'

The music of Jimi Hendrix (1942-70) experienced a

major revival. For many Hard Rock practitioners of the eighties, Hendrix was 'the king', his less-than-photogenic features plastered over millions of walls. Hendrix had been an avid student of occult literature. He advocated a rediscovery of 'the ancient arts', including primal religion. His definition of pagan practice owed much to his reading of the works of Aleister Crowley.

Before Hendrix took the stage for the last time, the announcement was made that his concert was aimed to build a bridge so that those listening might pass over to the nether world. Everyone was encouraged to chant the sacred OM sound. The blood-letting that resulted is a matter of record.

At Woodstock, Hendrix, along with The Who and Grateful Dead, had performed to 500,000 young people. The festival had been promoted as 'the Aquarian exposition'.[3]

Following the death of Hendrix, his cause was championed by the Rolling Stones and Grateful Dead. Mick Jagger believed that each time his group performed 'Sympathy for the Devil' they became possessed — and something 'very strange' happened in the audience. The death of Rolling Stone Brian Jones, of Hendrix, and of Janis Joplin, together with the break-up of the Beatles, dissipated, for a time, the concentration of evil that surrounded the Rock business. All this happened in the early seventies. But by the late seventies it was all back again. And the constant factor had been the group Grateful Dead.

It was Grateful Dead who attempted the Hendrix experiment amid the pyramids of Giza in 1978. Lead guitarist Phil Lesh believed that they were calling forth the ancient power represented by the pyramids. With thousands in the audience, he claimed to have experienced 'waves of spiritual power' through the music.[4]

Jim Morrison had believed that he was spirit-possessed, that he himself was a shaman and that this gave him the right to brutalize women. In 1970 he had married the priestess of a witches' coven in a Wicca wedding ceremony that involved invoking the presence of a Satanic 'goddess' and the mingling of blood.[5]

Black Sabbath, a British group, together with Ozzy Osbourne and AC/DC brought Black Metal and Death Metal from the seventies into the eighties with songs like 'Highway to Hell', 'Emperor Dark Throne' and 'Morbid Angel'. On the album cover 'Shout at the Devil', Tommy Lee wrote: 'The kids want something that's either gunna scare them or make their ears bleed, or make them happy. If you cover all three angles — man, you've got it locked up!'

Without doubt, the Black Metal bands thrived on negative publicity. Cloven Hoof actually issued a press release announcing that the group's name meant 'Followers at the feet of the devil'. The title track of their debut album was drawn out of a witchcraft document. Venom, another Black Metal group, sang songs with titles like 'Welcome to Hell', and 'In League with Satan'.

A price to pay. Steve Turner, in his history of Rock, writes: 'For those Rock and Roll people who danced too closely with the devil there was a price to pay.'[6] Brian Jones ended up dead in his own swimming pool. Jim Morrison died in a Paris bathtub. Graham Bond was crushed by the wheels of a London underground train. Led Zeppelin was brought to a halt by the sudden death of John Bonham (and Jimmy Page has remained a recluse ever since).

While Satanism had been a marketing ploy for some, for others, like Merciful Fate, Satanism was taken very seriously. In 'The Oath' they sang, 'I deny Jesus Christ the Deceiver/And abjure the Christian faith/Holding in contempt all of its works.' MDC's album 'Millions of Damn Christians' ridicules virtually every aspect of the Christian faith, life and revelation, more especially the blood of Christ.

The Rock lyrics of Billy Idol in 'White Wedding', and George Michael in 'Father Figure' similarly ridiculed the Cross. During the eighties there was, it would appear, an obsession with the Cross among Rock performers. The more blasphemous the artiste, the larger his jewelled cross. Prince actually sang an item called 'The Cross'. The spiritually naïve listened to his music, heard allusions to Christ, and believed that he must be some new breed of Christian. Raised in an American fundamentalist background, Prince did sing of heaven, hell, the devil and crucifixion. However, he managed to combine this with songs about fornication, voyeurism, masturbation and incest. His former bodyguard Chic Huntsbury said: 'He worships religion and sex. He's just a little confused over which one he likes best.'[7]

Nor was Prince by any means the only performer with a pagan-Christian tension in his work. Morrison's 'Avalon Sunset' (1989) was a lumpy mix of Christian and New Age ideas. By 1991, he was including traditional hymns — such as 'Be Thou My Vision' — in his albums. But the prevailing atmosphere is one of primal, pagan religion; 'the god within', 'the universal power that unites man and nature'.

Madonna. The performances of Madonna are, perhaps, the most obvious examples of the use of religious imagery in a totally carnal context.

In some performances a cross will be used as a background to sexual posing. In others it will be inverted (a symbol of Satanism through the centuries). This was a feature of the Rolling Stones' 1981 world tour and has appeared on the cover of a Duran Duran album.

Innumerable performers have injected religious elements into their outrageous acts, appealing to the public with names like Jesus Jones, Faith No More and MC 900 FT Jesus. In an album 'Born Again', Black Sabbath sang, 'The only good Christian is a dead Christian'. In the album called 'Welcome to Hell', the group Venom said, 'We're possessed by all that is evil/The death of You, God, we demand.' The Satan pentagram symbol occurs on many record sleeves, as well as the inverted cross. Toyah Wilcox, Ozzy Osbourne, Rick James, Meatloaf, Cheap Trick, Motley Crew, Coven and Kiss are performers/groups habitually using an obscure hand gesture that is the symbol of Satan. This hand gesture is, needless to say, copied by their thousands of fans.[8]

Occult ritual abounds in the lyrics of King Diamond, Merciful Fate, Black Sabbath and Possessed.

Demons on stage. Bauhaus was very much a fringe Heavy Metal group, typical of many others. In one performance, Peter Murphy of Bauhaus recited repeatedly the Latin for 'Father, Son and Holy Spirit', both forwards and backwards. This created an atmosphere that could be cut by a knife. The following description of that performance subsequently appeared in *Propaganda* magazine: 'Peter summoned his last reserves for the final push. As if suddenly possessed by demons, the whole foul-smelling mess spouted from his mouth like so much vomit. . . . Later the lingering evil spirits literally chased them right out of the dark studio, causing them to glance over their shoulders and laugh nervously as they spilled out into the street.'

Ozzy Osbourne sang a song entitled 'Mr Crowley'. The group Celtic Frost dedicated an album to 'The Great Magician' (whom they identified as Aleister Crowley). The British Rock group Psychic TV, the musical voice of an occult sect, adulates Aleister Crowley and virtually every other prominent Satanist.[9]

Rap. While knowing nothing of Satanism, Reggae represents the musical face of Rastafarianism and, hence, a mix of the religious and the profane. Similarly, Rap, in so far as it has any philosophy behind it, reflects the Nation of Islam (which now has mosques or temples in 120 American cities). Among the Rap groups supporting the Nation of Islam are Lench Mog and Public Enemy.

In the *US News and World Report*, Rap, along with Heavy Metal, is attacked for 'shocking indecency'. In a recent British analysis, Rap is given the credit for 'taking a stand against such things as child abuse and the misuse of drugs'. Nevertheless, on the flip side, Rap is accused of associating sex with violence and, in particular, of 'a hatred of women', and 'language calculated to demean women and promote their exploitation as sex objects'.[10]

In his article, 'The Corruption of Rock', Michael Medved asserts that 'the worst attitudes towards women are displayed by some of the Rap musicians. In Rap culture, terms like "my bitch" or "my whore" are habitually used to describe girlfriends. One of the worst offenders among the Rap musicians is NWA . . . .' Nevertheless, says Medved, the album in which NWA expose their worst excesses 'Nasty as they Wanna be' sold more than 1.7 million copies.[11] In Florida it was ruled obscene by a judge, who asserted that its central theme was the mutilation of the genitals of female partners.

Bob Demoss in *Focus on the Family*, analysing the same album, said that in less than sixty minutes there were 226 uses of the 'F' word, 163 uses of the word 'bitch', 87 descriptions of oral sex, and 117 explicit terms for male and female genitalia. Black writers have been outspoken in expressing their concern about the negative influence of certain Rap lyrics, and the violence implicit in the work of prominent US and UK cult rappers.[12]

Absorbing the Satanist and obscene content of Hard Rock, Heavy Metal and Rap music over a period of years would leave a lot of 'garbage' in the subconscious that a drug like LSD might bring into the conscious mind. 'I never stress the pernicious power of *one* movie, or one TV show, or one hit song,' writes Michael Medved. 'What concerns me is the accumulated impact of irresponsible messages that are repeated hour after hour, year after year . . . .'

But what about the end of the Rock spectrum — Kerrang, Thrash Metal, Rave — where there are no lyrics? Are lyrics the only means whereby damage can be done to physical and mental health?

[1]Andre Nataf, *Dictionary of the Occult* (Wordsworth, 1994), page 121. [2]Steve Turner, op cit, pages 92-95. [3]Ibid, pages 96, 97, 99, 100, 103, 104. [4]Ibid, pages 104, 106, 120-122. [5]Ibid, page 95. [6]Ibid, pages 99, 100; Bob and Gretchen Passantino, *When the Devil Dares Your Kids* (Eagle, 1996), pages 106, 108-114. [7]Eric Holmberg, *Hell's Bells: The Dangers of Rock and Roll* (Reel to Real Video). [8]Michael Medved, 'The Corruption of Rock', *The Sunday Times*, 28 February 1994; Eric Barger, *From Rock to Rock* (Huntingdon House, 1990). [9]David Kotzebue, *The Rock that Doesn't Roll* (1992). [10]*The Independent on Sunday*, 4 February 1996. [11]*The Sunday Times*, 28 February 1993. [12]Nathan McCall, 'How Rap's Hate Lyrics Harm Youngsters', *Reader's Digest* (August 1994), pages 88-92; *The Sunday Times*, 21 April 1996; Passantino, op cit, pages 108-114.

'You can hypnotize with music'

'I don't know which will go first,' remarked John Lennon, 'Rock 'n' Roll or Christianity . . . .'

First wave. Brought up in the evangelical South, the early, pre-Beatles Rock stars had recognized the tension between Rock and Christianity. Lennon was to follow Rock into drugs and the New Age counter-culture, spending his final years in 'a painted desert'. But Rock pioneers like Presley, Little Richard and Jerry Lee Lewis stopped well short of gurus.

Lewis never shook off the feeling that Rock, by its very nature, was 'the devil's music', believing that it had ruined his life. Little Richard wrote, 'A lot of the beats in music today are taken from voodoo, from the voodoo drums. If you study music and rhythms, as I have, you will see that it's true. I believe that kind of music is driving people from Christ. It is contagious. I believe that God wants people to turn from Rock 'n' Roll to the Rock of Ages.'[1]

Where's the harm? Steve Russo, a Rock star who turned to Christianity, went to some lengths to establish a connection between changes in popular culture — more especially the movies and Rock — and changes in patterns of behaviour over the last thirty years. He cited studies that demonstrated that the average student listened to 10,000 hours of music between the seventh and twelfth grades, quite apart from the thousands of hours watching TV. However, for Russo, the danger of Rock was exclusively in the message contained in the lyrics. Where the themes of sex, violence, rebellion, suicide and the occult were dominant, he argued, a negative impact on behaviour was inevitable.[2]

Eric Holmberg's exhaustive study of twenty years of Rock also concentrated on lyrics and imagery, together with the lifestyle of the Rock idols.[3]

Top-of-the-news court cases since the mid-eighties, however, have drawn attention to the *nature of the music*, as well as to the content of the lyrics.

Heavy Metal Rocker Ozzy Osbourne, several of his associates, and the company that produced his albums found themselves in the dock in a series of court cases in which the parents of suicide victims sought to prove their culpability for the suicide deaths of teenagers. The Institute for Bio-Acoustics Research was hired to evaluate Ozzy's 'Suicide Solution' song. The tape was played in court and the representatives of IBAR said, 'If you concentrate, you'll hear a heartbeat moving quite fast. That's designed to key into your own heartbeat and make it move faster.' In addition, IBAR discovered 'vocal fills and ad libs' that contained subliminal messages. These had been sung at one-and-a-half times the normal rate of speech. When these were reiterated again and again, it was argued, they inevitably produced a reaction . . . .

When the Heavy Metal Rock group Judas Priest found itself in court following the suicide of a teenager, they, too, found that the court was as interested in the nature of their music as in the content of their lyrics. The bill of complaint stated that, 'the suggestive lyrics combined with the continuous beat and rhythmic non-changing intonation of the music combined to induce, encourage, aid, abet and otherwise mesmerize the plaintiff into believing that the answer to life was death'. The suicide's mother stated in court that her son had taken his own life after 'a marathon Heavy Metal session'.[4]

There can be little doubt that Russo was wrong in his belief that the only evil in Rock was in the lyrics.

What's going on? Those who have examined the 'Techno Pagan' 'Festy Rave' scene of the nineties have, like Little Richard, identified dangers in the nature of the music itself. In the Rave scene there are no lyrics to analyse!

Pat Pulling's study of the effects of Heavy Metal and Black Metal music concentrates on the frequency of the sound waves that lead individuals to a loss of self-control. The US military, she argues, has made use of this knowledge for decades. She cites the work of Lieutenant Colonel Michael Aquino: 'ELF- (Extremely Low Frequency) waves (up to 100 Hz) are naturally occurring, but can also be produced artificially. ELF-waves are not normally noticed by the unaided senses, yet their resonant effect upon the human body has been connected to both psychological disorders and emotional distortion. Infrasound vibration (up to 20 Hz) can subliminally influence brain activity to align itself to Delta, Theta, Alpha or Beta wave patterns, inclining an audience towards everything from alertness to passivity. Infrasound could be used tactically, as ELF-waves endure for great distances; and it could be used in conjunction with media broadcasts as well.'[5]

Music can, apparently, affect the listener both physiologically and psychologically, manipulating and distorting the thinking processes. The experts tell us that this can, in particular, pose a serious threat to the psychological, emotional and physical wellbeing of teenagers and young adults.

An attorney's view. A top-flight American attorney studied the court cases brought against Rock groups/ stars between 1985 and 95. He also made use of expert analysis of not only the actual songs being brought into question, but the whole genre of which they were a part. The attorney concluded, 'The body is a dynamic bundle of many rhythms: heartbeat, respiration, even brain-waves. Like music, we are rhythmical, and as the body senses a rhythm in its environment, it adapts to it, accepting the mood that it conveys . . . .'

He goes on to contrast the psychological impact of music in which the rhythm is predictable, with heavy/hard Rock music in which the beat is changed. He persuasively demonstrates that the latter kind of music produces psychological disorientation.[6]

The Hendrix claim. Almost thirty years previously, Jimi Hendrix had taken the same view — and then had gone on to make much more astonishing assertions.

In a magazine interview, Hendrix had said that once Rock had achieved the primary disorientating effect the music became inherently manipulative. 'You can hyp-notize with music,' he said, 'and when you get people at the weakest point, you can preach into the subconscious what you want to say . . . .'[7]

[1]Steve Turner, op cit, pages vii, 3-28. [2]Steve Russo, *The Devil's Playground* (Harvest House, 1994), pages 18-20, 45-47, 72-76. [3]Eric Holmberg, *Hell's Bells: The Dangers of Rock and Roll* (Reel to Real Video). [4]Bob and Gretchen Passantino, *When the Devil Dares Your Kids* (Eagle, 1996), 118, 119. [5]Pat Pulling (with Kathy Cawthon), *The Devil's Web: Who is Stalking Your Children?* (Word, 1990), page 109. [6]Lewis R. Walton, *Omega II* (Self published, 1995), page 81. [7]Hendrix Interview, *Life* magazine, 2 October 1969.

Rave New World

Jimi Hendrix made his famous you-can-manipulate-behaviour-through-Rock claim twenty years before 'Techno Pagan' and 'Rave'.

Joni Mitchell, a seventies pop veteran wrote in *Rolling Stone* magazine in 1991: 'Music has become a burlesque over the last few years. . . . Every generation has to be more shocking than the last. . . . Our country is going down the tubes from it. It's rotten to the core.' Even the Rolling Stones, he argued, were 'sentimental softies' by comparison with contemporary Rave groups.

Inducing the trance state. The Techno Pagan/Festy Rave scene represented, he argued, a merger of the hedonism of the Rave culture and the radical Right wing politics and New Age philosophies of the post-punk groups. The result was a dance culture with its roots in Shamanism, and the power of music to alter consciousness. The altered consciousness of the sixties had been drug induced; the Rave culture could achieve a more devastating effect by sound alone (although, he conceded, no one in his right mind went to a Rave without topping up with chemicals). The Acid House sound depended on the Roland TBR303 baseline machine 'with tweaked samples to create a hypnotic effect' — first used in Chicago in the late eighties — together with the electronics of Europe and the rhythms of Detroit. This had first been tried in 1988, when empty buildings and far-flung spaces had been commandeered by giant sound systems and light shows, and a crowd of up to 5,000 had taken part in a massive all-night Rave in Britain's 'summer of love'. LSD and Ecstasy, with the psychedelic amphetamine MDMA, had been the drugs of choice. This had been the first of many all-night Raves, and the pattern for the rest.

A non-participating observer of a number of early Raves, Nicholas Saunders, reports: 'The combination of the drugs with music and dancing together produces an exhilarating trance-like state, perhaps similar to that experienced in tribal rituals or religious ceremonies. . . . In an ideal Rave, the drugs and the music would work to the same end — that of giving those in the crowd the illusion of being part of a single pulsating organism. The drugs slowly blurred the distinctions of the real and the unreal, the "me" and the "them", while the high decibel music with its hypnotic 140-160 beats per minute reprogrammes the consciousness.'[1]

'The birth canal of the New Age.' From being an observer, Saunders decided to experiment as a Rave participant. He began by taking Ecstasy. He then goes on to describe the gradual loss of all restraint to a point at which he 'melted into' the vast crowd. In the moving mass, he said, all were, nevertheless, 'separately celebrating in their own space'. There was no body contact or eye contact, and no verbal interchange whatsoever. It was his perception that the Rave sound was produced by a computer-literate generation with no moral qualms. With others, he believed that he was witnessing the birth of the ultimate counter-culture that would, early in the next millennium, facilitate the birth of the New Age that would bury the 'Christian monotheistic mind state'. The 'new religion' would be one in which everyone would have his 'familiar'; the last vestiges of the 'barrier to the beyond' would be dissolved; and mass Raves would take the place of worship.[2]

So what is the future of 'Britpop', the likes of Blurr and Oasis?

It depends upon which magazine you read. The avid

Rave fanatic believes in the dictum 'Rave conquers all', and 'Commercial pop' will be subsumed beneath it before long.

Others see (and hear) in Britpop enough resonances of Beatle-mania from the sixties to make them believe that it is the beginning of a longer-term conditioning of earliteens, preparatory to eventual graduation to Rave.

When you emerge from Rave. . . . Articles published in *The Journal of Music Therapy* in 1992 and 1993 have argued that the whole purpose of 'Techno' and 'Rave' is to alter consciousness. This altered consciousness takes place, in part, as a direct result of the chemical effects of the drugs made necessary by the all-night sessions and, partly, as a result of the intrinsic nature of the Rave sound itself. The disorientation was only the start . . . .

Psychologist Dr George Stevenson, in *Music and Your Emotions*, argued that it was almost impossible to exaggerate 'the great psychological force' that was music. Advertisers with their sound tracks and jingles, and retailers with their musak had acknowledged it for years. The researches cited by Stevenson, carried out over several decades, demonstrate the effect of music on the human mind and body.

Blood chemistry and heartbeat. Evidence is produced that music actually affects the body's blood chemistry. Chemical changes are some of the most fundamental ways the body governs itself. The fact that music can produce changes there indicates that it is a major catalyst for change in both brain and body.

Putting aside 'Techno Pagan' and 'Rave' — thunderingly loud noises that dominate the mind and replace thought with instinct — Stevenson examines human reaction to music that the individual is not consciously aware of. This type of music can bypass those portions of the brain where conscious thought and judgement occur, and can go directly into the human organism through a part of the brain that responds to emotion and feeling. From there it can produce powerful effects.

Amplify the music by many times, until it shudders a body-packed enclosure, and it provokes almost irresistible urges. The heartbeat quickens in time to the percussive rhythm. The drone of the drumbeat moulds a mass of people into a single unit.

A heavy, iterative, rhythmic beat has an effect very similar to hypnosis. It has been clinically demonstrated that it intensifies our emotions and can alter our normal behaviour patterns.

There is, apparently, a direct relationship between the music experienced and, say, a subsequent homicide or suicide, especially if the perpetrator/victim is a young person. Young adulthood, it is argued, is the period of transition during which an individual is moving among a variety of value systems, searching for his/her niche. In these circumstances, the disorientation, cancellation of thought, and reduction to primal urges produced by Heavy Metal/Rave can provide an environment in which the mind is either 'broken' or, if there are lyrics or subliminal messages, opened to nihilism, sensualism, Satanism, or, for that matter, any other ism or wasm.

Decibels. Arguably the best medical research on the impact of heavy beat, anapaestic rhythm and high decibels on the human brain and body was published ten years before the advent of Rave.[3]

A Channel 4 documentary 'Rave New World', put out on 6 November 1994, drew on this research, but added to it more recent observation undertaken since the advent of Rave.

The programme presenters measured the sound output of an all-night Rave at 100,000 watts (150 decibels), equivalent to the sound of a space shuttle taking off!

Given that permanent damage to hearing can be inflicted by any sound of 100 decibels and above, the most obvious physical consequence of Rave was hearing impairment. 'It pounds the ear with a relentless 4/4 rhythm of up to 180 beats a minute from the moment you enter the Rave . . . .'[4]

In the context of a Rave, to the disorientation and body-chemical effects produced by the tantric rhythm must be added the impossibility of thought and the removal of normal constraints on behaviour. Add to this the effects of hard drugs, exhaustion and the dehydration produced by all-night sessions, and all that is left of the individual is a very basic primal instinct.

But even that is not the end of the story. Stabbing through the blackness, and adding to the disorientation of the all-encompassing din, is photic lighting.

Strobes. It is through correlating the frequency of the strobe shafts with the percussion beats that Rave achieves maximum impact on the brain. The rhythmic stimulation of both sound and lighting affects 'many sensory and motor areas of the brain, not ordinarily affected'. Agitated behaviour begins when the percussion-light frequency reaches eight or nine cycles per second. As the frequency increases, so the sound-and-light source begins to 'drive' behaviour in a most alarming fashion. The subjects — dancers — can be 'driven' towards a whole range of emotions and reactions, including fear, disgust, anger, pleasure — and violence. At a relatively early stage, a hallucinatory effect is achieved. In researches, 'the hallucinations described by subjects were of a character so compelling that one subject was able to sketch them some weeks later'.

On a more mundane, but potentially devastating level, 'over-breathing' or 'hyperventilating' takes place. 'Low blood glucose and production of adrenalin, which results from over-exertion and fatigue', further increases susceptibility to the rhythm of light and sound. This places the subject/dancer in a perilous condition, both physically and mentally. In one piece of scientific research a dancer, responding to the rhythm, began 'dancing uncontrollably and most energetically until she fell into a clairvoyant trance . . . '.

Professor A. Neher in 'Physiological explanations of unusual behaviour', *Human Biology* (volume 35) pages 151-160, continues his description of an experiment equivalent to a 'mild' Rave: 'The dance . . . consists of very forcible rhythmic undulating movements of the whole head and torso. The arms are jerked forcibly backwards so that the elbows nearly meet, the knees are slightly bent, and the dancer goes round in circles with small shuffling steps while making these violent, physical movements.' After a long period of such dancing, a 'clairvoyant trance' may be achieved or, alternatively, the dancer may fall to the ground in a 'cataleptic fit'. 'Almost all subjects, including normal subjects, show both brainwave changes and report unusual subjective feelings to rhythmic light stimulation. . . . The amount of self-control that such subjects can exercise is limited and the experimenters must be careful to terminate the stimulus before an unwanted convulsion occurs . . . .'[5]

'Photic driving' — a combination of loud percussive sound and light — can render the subject entirely helpless and vacuous, a prey to whatever power or force or message his/her manipulator may wish to inflict.

Hence, according to sound scientific research, the conditions produced in the average Rave are capable of opening the subject (victim) to control in a way not dreamt of by the totalitarian dictators of past decades.

That Techno Paganism and Rave might prove the

birth canal of New Age diabolic control, even if only for a segment of the younger generation, has to be a subject of serious concern.

As Mr C. of The Shamen Rave group told Ben Thompson of *Independent on Sunday* (4 February 1996), 'There's a definite magic to be found in the rhythms. It's scientific knowledge that Alpha and Theta waves are altered by percussive sounds and light. And that throws you into an altered state of consciousness, releasing the neurons in getting you completely out there, which is connecting to something that some people call Gaia, and some people call God, but whatever you call it, it's big, and it's powerful . . . .'

Mr C, real name Richard West, 30, believes that the shadowy gang of spaced-out techno-mystics called The Shamen are modern-day equivalents of those in past centuries who have talked with the spirits . . . .

---

[1]Nicholas Saunders, *E For Ecstasy* (Self-published, London 1993). [2]Ibid; T. McKenna, *The Archaic Revival* (HarperCollins, 1991). [3]John Diamond, MD, *Behavioural Kinesiology* (Harper and Rowe, 1979), page 101. [4]'Rave New World', (Equinox), Channel Four, 6 November 1994. [5]Andrew Neher, 'A physiological explanation of unusual behaviour in ceremonies involving drums', *Human Biology*, volume 34, pages 151-160.

Note. Andrew Neher is a Professor of Anthropology. His researches were first published as early as 1962. In addition to details of his experiments in laboratory conditions, his excellent article contains accounts of Rave-like phenomena in primitive societies, including Haiti and Central Africa. We are deeply indebted to his researches.

Is there a Verdict?

The death obsession of the Rock and Rave scene of the early nineties alone could account for Justin's suicide, but not quite . . . .

The chemical effects of 100-plus doses of LSD — including the introduction to the conscious of the Rock-struck garbage (and latent neuroses) from the sub-conscious mind — alone could account for Justin's suicide, but there would still be questions . . . .

Attendance at a series of all-night Raves — sound at 150 decibels, music at a hypnotic 140-160 beats per minute — 'reprogrammed' his consciousness, rendering him wide open to any force or influence imaginable. The impact upon the brain of synchronized rhythmic beat and stabs of bright light — eight or nine cycles a second over four, five, six hours — could 'drive' his behaviour through paranoia and violence to hallucination and 'clairvoyant trance'. And that, added to the nihilistic messages and the psychological consequences of bingeing on LSD, brings us close to a verdict . . . .

But what about the voices?

Yes, 'voices' could result from a schizophrenic tendency latent in the subconscious, brought to the conscious mind as a result of LSD. Yes, 'voices' could be part of the consequence of hallucinatory and trance behaviour 'driven' into a particularly sensitive, vulnerable mind by Rave . . . .

But even this could not quite account for the voices that Justin heard . . . . The black-garbed figures adding hypnotic stares to a hypnotic sound-light rhythm . . . . Then the inverted cross circled in blood from his own veins, and the series of occult symbols: 'If you are

receptive to our powers, you will receive a thump' . . .
the detailed, profoundly evil threats and instructions . . .
the final instruction to inhale water . . . the apparent
suicide of a near-19-year-old who had begun to emerge
from drugs and Rave, and to get in cahoots with his
Christian roots, and to contemplate the bright uplands
of hope . . . .

'Spirit' voices? And we find ourselves in the Swedenborg, Conan Doyle, Fox family world of the spirits . . .
the heavy penumbra on the edge of New Age where dark
forces abound and 'dead spirits' are channelled: the
world inhabited by so many Rock and Rave bands of the
eighties and nineties, whether we take their expressions
of loyalty to Satan and their use of Satanic symbols and
their abuse of Christ and Christian symbols as deliberate
or as part of an assumed image. . . . And Rave, say the
insiders, is the birth canal of the New Age in which
everyone will have his 'familiar', and the last barriers to
'the Beyond' will have been dissolved . . . .

So what is 'the Beyond' of Blavatsky? Who are 'the
entities' variously described as 'the masters' or 'the
spirits'?

Since they would appear to hold the key not only to
Justin's suicide but to the powerful impact of Hard
Rock, Heavy Metal, Techno Pagan and Rave, perhaps
they also hold the key to much else in a world which, at
times, seems almost overwhelmed with evil . . . .

What are 'the spirits' that rap and chatter and inform
the utterances of the whole kit-and-caboodle of spiritualists, astrologers, channellers, witches, New Agers, clair-
voyants, soothsayers, Satanists — the whole spook-
besotted crew?

Is 'the Beyond' death, and are 'the spirits' dead
people?

Cherie's story. Cherie says an emphatic, 'No!' And she should know.

Cherie started life with the chips stacked against her. Both of her parents were alcoholics before she and her twin sister, Madeleine, were born. They were brought up in France. Cherie recollects that as a small child she often carried bottles home for her mother. . . . Cherie and her twin sister were just two of a family of eight.

Childhood for Cherie and her twin was one long nightmare. Alcohol was the fuel, and the spirits the spark that ignited the father's uncontrollable rages. These rages were generally turned upon Cherie's mother, but from time to time would impact upon any member of the family. But the father reserved his worst violence for his wife, and sometimes his powerful fists occasioned actual bodily harm and she had to be rushed into hospital.

An obsession with astrology may have been the door through which the spirits entered the home. There may have been an occult involvement outside the home. But adding to the constant static in the atmosphere there was something evil. There were psychic assaults, and psychic phenomena. Cherie's only friend was her twin sister. They were very close. On two occasions, they actually ran away from home because they could take no more. But, at heart, they craved their parents' love above everything, and they always came back . . . .

As teenagers they experimented with ouija boards. . . . The circle of letters, the 'Yes' and the 'No' and, in the centre, the glass. . . . At first it seemed a fun thing; though it was somewhat unnerving when, in response to the questions they had addressed to 'the spirit of the glass', the glass actually moved to provide an answer. . . . It was Cherie who asked the question,

'When shall I die?' and watched the glass spell out the answer, 'Before your next birthday.'

Then, terror. Terror; and depression.[1] Cherie had always been aware that along with most of her siblings she had inherited from her parents a weakness for alcohol.

Even when the ouija board had been burned, the answer to the last question Cherie had addressed to it hung over her head like a death sentence.

As soon as she reached 15, Cherie left home. Despite her tendency towards alcoholism, she had a keen interest in health and physical fitness. Hence she had enrolled at a school specializing in sport. At the school, physical fitness was all.

At weekends Cherie was obliged to return to her family. While there was much in her home from which she would dearly have liked to escape, there was also Madeleine, with whom she had a close relationship. During the week she found that she missed the company of her sister so much that, at the end of the first academic year, Cherie quit school and returned home.

Hard Rock. At the school Cherie had become involved in the Hard Rock scene and returned home a 'Heavy Metal kid'. 'I did not know at that time,' she told me, 'that my studded leather jacket and my boots were just a shield to protect me from the outside world. I felt so frail inside . . . .'

Back home, Cherie's relationship with her sister changed when boyfriends came on the scene. She failed to understand that her sister needed her own space; and that this was more important to her than her close relationship with her twin.

Cherie found a new circle of friends. She would spend whole weekends with them. It was not long before she was heavily into alcohol, the Heavy Metal dance scene, and was smoking marijuana.

Looking back, Cherie says it was 'a love substitute'. 'We got into anorexia for a few months, but nobody really cared,' she told me. 'Sometimes I felt so distressed that I thought of committing suicide.'

Things were getting worse at home, coming to a climax. During this period her father did things that she would find very hard to forgive in the future. But her bad relationship was no longer just with her father; it was with her twin sister, too.

At the age of 17, Cherie left home for the second time and crossed the Channel to England to work for five months as an *au pair*. Keen on languages, she began to brush up on her English.

On her return to France, there could be no question of going back home to live. Cherie went to stay with the family with whom she had lived during her period at the sports school. She found that the mother and daughter were Protestant Christians. After passing her university entrance examinations, she took a part-time job as a secretary.

Cherie had received no religious education whatever and had never read any Christian books. Her mother had been a nominal Catholic, whereas her father had been an atheist.

Cherie says, 'My life was like a burden; my heart was full of hatred, bitterness and sorrow, which made me sick. I binged on sweet things and ended up with hypoglycaemia, as well as putting on weight!'

Books in the barn. Influenced by her surrogate family, Cherie began to think of God. No sooner had she begun her search for God than in the barn she discovered a box of books. She picked out a couple, and in secret began to read them.

As Cherie read, she began to move towards a belief in God's existence. She also became convinced that the Bible was God's revelation to man.

From reading books, Cherie began to read the Book of books.

She found that fundamental to Scripture and to life was a conflict of kingdoms. There was, she discovered, the kingdom of God and the kingdom of Satan . . . .

It was all there at the beginning of Genesis:

• Only God had been there 'in the beginning', all supreme. At that time there had been no clash of kingdoms. 'In the beginning' there had been neither Satan nor man.

• God had created the heavens before the earth, and the heavenly realm had been populated by angelic beings. This was the supernatural realm. For all that, the angels were created beings, *not* on a par with their Creator.

• Rebellion had taken place in the supernatural realm. Though the angelic Lucifer (Satan) had been given a powerful position in heaven, he had resolved 'to be like the Most High'. Satan was going for God! He was set on a strategy of defaming the character of God. And his strategy was successful to the extent that one third of the heavenly host became followers of Satan. Then there was war in heaven.[2] As a result, before the dawn of earth time, a great inter-galactic war had been fought. Lucifer (Satan) and his followers had been cast out of heaven — and earth had become the theatre of war. Jesus, the Son of God, had seen Satan 'fall like lightning from heaven'.[3] In God's kingdom there was room for but one throne; and in human life there is room for but one King.

• God then made man, His earthly, non-supernatural creation. But Satan, cast out of heaven, did not lose his supernatural abilities, nor did the angels-cum-demons cast out with him. Not long after the beginning of earth-time, they began to target man.

Demons look for doors. To Cherie, all this clarified a great deal. Satan, using a speaking serpent as medium, had brought about the fall of man and all of its consequences: suffering, pain, war, disease, and all of which man, under the control of evil, is capable.

Cherie discovered that the angels-turned-demons — intelligent, observant, supernatural — were all too willing to become involved in human lives when invited by occult dabblers — and then to introduce the terrors of hell into homes. This made sense of psychic phenomena in her parents' home. She realized that there were all kinds of doorways into a human life that demons could use: ouija boards, astrology, occult practices like levitation, all kinds of 'magic', psychic counselling, channelling, mediumship, TM and Yoga (both of which she had encountered in her Heavy Metal experience), and even certain kinds of films, books and magazines. . . . She discovered that dabbling with Spiritualism, witchcraft and Satanism, whether seriously or lightheartedly, was to throw one's life wide open to demons.

And Cherie discovered that throughout Scripture God had taken the firmest possible line against the evil supernatural. There were two supernatural kingdoms; one was God's and one was Satan's. And God wanted man to know, right from the start, the doorways that Satan's evil empire would use to gain access to human lives. Out of hand, God condemned the pagan practices of divination, sorcery, child sacrifice, the interpretation of omens, all aspects of witchcraft, spells, mediums, channellers, spiritists. 'Anyone who does these things is detestable to the Lord.'[4]

A clash of kingdoms. If Cherie could discover from these things much that made sense of certain aspects of her own life, we can, perhaps, gain an insight into the missing link in Justin's tragic story.

Justin had been involved in a clash of kingdoms. In the conflict that had ensued, he had opened doors to his mind and life: through drugs and Rave. In the concluding weeks of the boy's life, his father had taken him through the Scriptural passages that Cherie was to find in the Bible she discovered in a French barn. From his Christian background Justin had, from the first time he heard his 'voices', identified their source as Ultimate Evil. As his father worked through the Bible passages with him, his faith was confirmed, as was his determination to close the doors tight shut. He had begun to pray again, and to read about the Gospel of salvation. He had spent the last evening of his life doing just that. And that had made Satan desperate.

God is invincible. Doubtless, Satan was desperate when Cherie found the books in the barn, began to read them and to absorb the Gospel of Christ.

In her studies, Cherie discovered that though humans are no match for Satan, Satan is no match for humans who have a relationship with God. Throughout the writings of Christianity's great champion, Paul, she discovered the phrase 'in Christ' and the promises that those 'in Christ' are proof against every supernatural enemy. 'In Christ', she discovered, meant accepting Christ as Saviour, His death on the cross for her sins.[5]

When Cherie hit on James 4:7, she underlined it heavily in her newly-discovered Bible: 'Give yourselves . . . to God. Resist the devil and he will flee from you.' Living Bible.

God is supreme, all powerful. When those 'in Christ' who have submitted their lives to God resist Satan — Satan must flee. Why? Because Satan's actions take place within boundaries God has defined, established, and which He enforces.

So, 'Who shall separate us from the love of Christ? . . . I am convinced that neither death nor life, neither angels *nor demons*, neither the present nor the future, nor any powers, neither height nor depth, nor anything else in all creation, will be able to separate us from the love of God that is in Christ Jesus our Lord.'[6]

When Cherie reached that verse she whooped for joy!

'Then', she told me, 'something really extraordinary happened to me one December night in 1984 . . . .'

---

[1] In November 1994 a British judge dismissed a jury for using a ouija board, and restarted the trial. During the ensuing weeks almost every serious London newspaper used teams of investigative journalists to analyse ouija-related phenomena. All turned up evidence of terrifying paranormal phenomena and, with it, consequential depression and psychiatric disorder. *The Sunday Times: Style and Family Life*, 27 November 1994. [2] Revelation 12:4, 7, 8; Isaiah 14:13, 14. See Ezekiel chapter 28. [3] Luke 10:18; Isaiah 14:12; Jude 6; Revelation 12:7-9. [4] Deuteronomy 18:9-13. [5] Romans 3:21-8:2; Ephesians 2:8-10. See Isaiah chapter 53. [6] Romans 8:35, 38-39, italics supplied.

Recalled to Life

It happened after Cherie had made her discovery in the barn, but before what she was reading in the books and in the Bible had fallen into place.

She was wide awake in bed, distressed and unable to sleep.

The ache that existed in her life as a result of the rift with Madeleine was only part of the problem. The clash of kingdoms was taking place over Cherie that night. The inbuilt craving for alcohol — the result of her being a child of alcoholic parents, and of her own abuse of the drug — was still very real. It seemed that entities from the fallen supernatural realm, hostile to good and God, were seeking to use the doors she had opened to her inner self to gain access and assume permanent control. The doors? Ouija, Heavy Metal, alcohol, unforgiveness.

Cherie felt her weakness.

Night conversation. She needed help from that other supernatural realm where light, not darkness; joy, not pain; peace, not turmoil; Christ, not Satan, reigned. And, suddenly, spontaneously, Cherie spoke: 'God, if you exist, *let me know.*'

Even before the sound of Cherie's voice had died upon the silence, she was overwhelmed by the strongest possible feeling of peace and comfort. 'It was God answering me, spiritual light shining into me,' she told me. 'I wept for a long time during this conversation with the Holy Spirit who spoke straight to my heart. His sweet voice told me to abandon my hatred towards my father and my twin sister, and to forgive them . . . .'

This she did, instantly. Then, and subsequently, she has looked upon forgiveness as a gift.

Cherie believes that her spiritual healing began with receiving that gift.

In what Cherie calls her 'conversation with the Holy Spirit', she confessed and repented of all the doors to her life which she had opened and through which she had enabled Satanic forces to gain access. She realized that those forces had exposed her to a sense of depression and bleakness which had, on more than one occasion, brought her to the very edge of suicide. She asked God to close those doors permanently, to rid her life of evil cravings and influences, and to lead her to His salvation through His truth.

In Scripture she had read that grace, faith and forgiveness, even repentance and salvation, are gifts from God. But until that time she felt that she had failed to reach out for those gifts, to co-operate with God's miracle.

Cherie had read in Scripture that we are forgiven as we forgive; that we forgive those who wrong us, not seven times but, in the words of Jesus, 'more like seventy times seven'.[1] But she had persisted in her unforgiveness; and unforgiveness had become bitterness; bitterness had become repressed anger; and repressed anger had become emotional and spiritual illness — and was about to become physical illness, too.

Unconditional love. She felt that the Holy Spirit was directing her to Jesus' parable of the unmerciful servant.[2] Thus far she had failed to understand, receive and live God's unconditional love, grace and forgiveness. For this reason she had failed to give out that unconditional love and grace and forgiveness in her relationships with others.

Jesus had begun His parable by telling the apostle Peter that there is no limit to God's forgiveness. The point of the parable was to illustrate WHY there is no limit.

A servant owed millions of pounds to his king. The figure quoted by Jesus was larger than the annual taxation for Judaea, Samaria and Galilee put together. This vast sum made a vital point: an individual's debt to God is so great that he can never pay it back.

The servant fell before his king and begged for mercy — of a sort. He actually asked for extra time to pay. Ridiculous! How could he *ever* pay off a debt so vast?

The servant's idea of forgiveness was one thing. The king's was another. He didn't give him more time to pay. *He cancelled the debt completely.*

But here is the crunch of the story. The servant could not accept the gift he was being offered. He behaved as if he had just been given an extension of time to pay. He found another servant who owed him a tiny amount of money, grabbed him by the throat and said, 'Pay up!' And when he couldn't, threw him into prison.

It seemed to Cherie that the two verses at the conclusion of the parable were very important.[3] Finding out that, despite his cancellation of the debt, his servant had nevertheless hounded a fellow servant for a smaller sum, the king threw him into gaol and turned him over to the torturers.

This was a real shocker! What did it mean? Then Cherie realized, from her own experience, who the torturers were: Guilt, Resentment, Striving, Anxiety. These were the four torturers that produced emotional and spiritual problems, warped personalities and caused the breakdown of relationships.

Like the servant in the story, Cherie knew that she must understand that her King had cancelled her entire debt. His hands had been pierced for the wrong things her hands had done. His feet had been spiked for the wandering paths her feet had trod. His brow had been thorn-crushed for the wrong thoughts her mind had harboured. His heart had been broken for the wrong things her heart had loved. And it had happened on Calvary. God's sinless Son had borne her sins upon the Cross so that, through the strange transaction at the heart of the Christian Gospel, she might receive the free gift of His perfect righteousness — *and* God's everlasting salvation.[4]

Up till that December night, Cherie had not been able to believe the wonderful good news. Because she had not been able to believe it, she had not been able to receive it. Because she had not been able to receive it, she had not been able to live it. And because she had not been able to live it, she had not been able to enjoy it. In her relationships with her family — more especially her father and her twin sister — she had behaved like the pardoned debtor who still believed that he had to scrimp and save in order to pay all that he owed. And her life had been given over to a tragic treadmill: performing, achieving, striving. She had sought to pay her own debt, to make her own atonement. And, because that is impossible, her life had been filled with hardness and bitterness, and the hordes of Satan had surrounded her.

Dealing with the past. On that night of nights, Cherie did very little sleeping. She reflected on the lives of the Bible characters about whom she had read. She found that most of them had one thing in common: A past to live down, a life to rebuild from shame and failure. Jacob the trickster — who became 'the father of the faithful'. Moses the murderer — who became the greatest leader of men the world has ever known. David the adulterer — who became 'a man after God's own heart'. Peter the coward — who became a courageous champion of Christ's Gospel. Mary the prostitute — who became the first individual to receive the greatest news the world has ever heard: 'He is risen!'

She knew that God was calling her back to life!

She remembered how the apostle Paul had listed the worst kinds of offenders in the city of Corinth — adulterers, perverts, thieves, rapists, swindlers, drunkards — and then had added: 'And such were some of you!' Then he had gone on to tell them that they had been washed by the blood of Calvary. That they had been justified, treated as if they had never sinned. That they were being healed through the power of the indwelling Holy Spirit.[5]

Cherie realized that she no longer wanted to be one of the walking wounded. She craved for a healed life through the power of God. She had been recalled to life, and now she wanted to live that life to God's great glory.

Calvary, she discovered, had been a total package. Total pardon and total righteousness in exchange for total repentance.

Dawn release. As dawn broke, Cherie realized that a vicious circle can become more vicious; the unaccepted become unaccepting, the ungraced become ungracious, the unforgiven unforgiving. She understood the message of Jesus: 'You have locked yourself in a prison of your own unforgiveness. Forgive and you will be forgiven; release and you will be released.'

Before breakfast she was up and active. In turn she sought out her father, her mother, her twin sister and then the other members of her family — pouring forth the love that God had poured into her; being reconciled to them as she had been reconciled to Him.

Pronounced incurable. In the ensuing two months it

would have been impossible for Cherie to be happier. But there was one throw-back to the days before she came to Christ that still had to be encountered. Years of anxiety, bitterness and unforgiveness had taken their toll — on her body.

It all started with pain in her colon. The diagnosis was Crohn's disease. This disease affects the intestines and is not curable.

Cherie told God that she was ready to live the life He wanted her to live and to glorify Him in health and in sickness. However, when she went to bed, she asked Him for healing. While praying, she felt a strange 'operation' taking place in her body. It was a brief sensation, but quite unmistakable. She told me, 'Words cannot describe what happened.' Afterwards she fell asleep with the assurance that she had received God's healing. The next morning, all pain was gone and it has never returned.

She told her friends that she had been restored to life. They hardly needed telling because it was so obvious. One of her closest friends became a Christian a year later.

At the beginning of 1986, her hypoglycaemia was still with her. But God had a plan for that, too. For three weeks she stayed in a health centre in the south-west of France. During that three-week period far more than her hypoglycaemia was cured. The small evangelical church she had joined had been a block rather than a conduit for the grace and truth of God. In the health centre she learned of a new and better way. She embraced the full message of the Bible and, in 1987, with her friend, she was baptized by immersion. She felt that her baptism was a re-enactment of the death, burial and resurrection of Jesus. She had died with Christ; her old life a thing of the past. She was buried with Him; her sins and self-life buried, never to be exhumed, unless by her choice.

And, most glorious of all, she had risen with Christ — to new life, the risen life.[6]

Only a few months later her brother Francois was baptized. For some time her parents were hostile to what she had done; Protestants are a tiny minority in France. But when they saw the evidence of Cherie's new life in Christ, they were convinced.

Madeleine. For ten years after that, Cherie struggled and wept in prayer for her sister Madeleine. Her sister had become a single mother with two sons, the elder one being mentally handicapped.

Eventually, in 1993, joy of joys, Madeleine, too, was 'recalled to life'. Now, at 31, Cherie is completing her degree in English, Spanish and German at a French university. She plans to be a translator. And in her last letter from home there was evidence that her parents were moving towards the Gospel that has thrilled her and changed her life. Cherie acknowledges that alcoholism, drugs and Heavy Metal are merely a means to self-destruction. 'The devil hides out!' she says. 'With him appearances are always deceptive. All of his gimmicks have an attractive outside — but inside there is a yawning emptiness that consumes and, eventually, destroys.

'Most people don't start mainlining on heroin right away; they start with marijuana. That's how it is with the occult and the New Age. Some of the doorways into the devil's domain seem pretty harmless or, perhaps, even attractive; but that's not the issue. Where is the power coming from? How is Satan going to use that doorway?

'Astrology/mediumship are Satan's counterfeits for God's gift of prophecy. Get involved in those things and you are allowing Satan to mainline into your brain.[7]

'In the same way, ouija boards are tapping into the Satanic realms; and they bring terror, not truth.

'TM and the various kinds of Yoga are just other means to the Satanic supernatural. By chanting the mantra you are calling on an alien ''god'' force.

'And, as for Spiritualism and New Age channelling — they are the most dangerous delusions of all . . . .'

---

[1]See Matthew 18:22. [2]Matthew 18:23-35. [3]Matthew 18:34, 35. [4]2 Corinthians 5:21; 1 Peter 2:22, 24. [5]1 Corinthians 6:10, 11. [6]Romans 6:1-10. [7]Isaiah 47:13, 14.

The Final Frontier

The high profile given to New Age occult practices by the movie and Rock industries has a flip side for Satan.

It was possible to ignore Conan Doyle's Spiritualists as a sideshow for weirdos. It was possible to laugh off Madame Blavatsky's blend of Hinduism, Buddhism and Spiritualism as a fanatical fringe (more especially since the high society glitterati tended to keep their involvement quiet . . .).

But Hollywood's headliners and the honchos of Rock and Rave have shoved mediumship and channelling towards the top of the 'Let's-Check-It-Out' agenda. With New Age luminaries like Shirley Maclaine, Benjamin Creme and Marilyn Ferguson trumpeting the imminent arrival of 'the Lord Maitreya', the advent of the age of Aquarius early in the new millennium and, its corollary, the burial of Christianity, it is, perhaps, inevitable that even the sleepiest of Christians should begin to sit up and take an interest. 'The coming Lord Maitreya', proclaims Creme, 'is a conflation of the Messiah expected by Jews, the returning Christ expected by Christians, the Imam Mahdi expected by Muslims, the Krishna expected by Hindus and the new Buddha expected by Buddhists.'

Demon spirits. The practice of mediumship-channelling and the widespread claims made regarding the voices/appearances of 'dead spirits' has Christian thinkers on the edge of their seats.

'Just because it's supernatural doesn't mean to say it's from God,' they say cautiously. And they're right.

The more courageous Christian writers have come right out and, quoting Revelation 16:14, have said, 'They are spirits of demons performing miraculous signs.'

Some of Christianity's best brains have gone to work to provide a more convincing answer to the question everyone, *but everyone* asks: 'So what exactly *does* happen to us when we die?' And the answers they've come up with have not rendered them popular in all circles!

John Wenham, John Stott, Philip Edgecumbe Hughes, Edward Fudge and Clark Pinnock have all gone into print, expressing concern about popular theology on heaven and hell, as has an Anglican study group.

So what have they turned up by way of biblical evidence on the subject? What light does the available evidence shed on the claim of mediums and channellers to be able to communicate with the dead?

Here we have space for only a sampling of verses:

• Deuteronomy 31:16. God is telling Moses: '"You are going to rest with your fathers . . . ."'

• Job 14:10-12, 21. '"Man dies and is laid low; he breathes his last and is no more. . . . So man lies down and does not rise; till the heavens are no more, men will not awake or be roused from their sleep . . . ."' Job goes on to insist that, after death, if a man's '"sons are honoured, he does not know it; if they are brought low, he does not see it."'

• Ecclesiastes 9:5, 6, 10. 'For the living know that they will die, but the dead know nothing. . . . Never again will they have a part in anything that happens. . . . In the grave, where you are going, there is neither working nor planning nor knowledge nor wisdom.'

• Daniel 12:2. The prophet, describing the end of the age, says, '"Multitudes who sleep in the dust of the earth will awake: some to everlasting life, others to shame and everlasting contempt."'

• In Psalm 6:5 King David is clear that the dead are not sentient. Speaking about the dead, Job (7:10) says,

'''He will never come to his house again; his place will know him no more.'''

• On two occasions, Jesus referred to death as a 'sleep' (Mark 5:39; John 11:6, 7, 11-14). On the second occasion, Jesus was referring to His friend Lazarus; '''Our friend Lazarus has fallen asleep; but I am going there to wake him up.''' When it was clear that His disciples had misunderstood Him, believing that 'he meant natural sleep' (John 11:13), 'he told them plainly, "Lazarus is dead"' (verse 14). Jesus used the opportunity to expound His apocalyptic teaching; '''I am the resurrection and the life. He who believes in me will live, even though he dies; and whoever lives and believes in me will never die.''' (Verse 25.)

• When the first Christian martyr had been stoned to death, it is recorded, 'he fell asleep' (Acts 7:60).

In that selection of verses, there is not much support for those claiming to have contacted 'the other side' by way of the psychic telephone. In fact, in all Scripture, there is not a crumb of comfort for the medium or the channeller. The book of Revelation makes particularly uncomfortable reading for such people. In the end-time age, it tells us, Satan will be aware that his time is running out, and will assume a more hands-on role on the surface of the planet (Revelation 12:12; 16:14).

It is quite clear, then, that the alien entities are, as Cherie discovered, demon spirits. Mischievous spirits with access to information about past and present and who, because of their evil stratagems, are able to hazard shrewd guesses about some things that will happen in the future. Spirits whose activities have been whipped up into a fury because they are aware that their time is short.

Remember the first words addressed by Katie Fox, aged 12, to the alien spirit inhabiting her home? 'Mr

Splitfoot, do as I do.' Thereafter she found that 'Mr Splitfoot' was a highly intelligent, alien being. However, in naming him thus, Katie displayed a shrewdness beyond her years. Her clear reference to the devil represents a psychic hole-in-one. Modern dabblers in the world of the occult would do well to heed the warning implicit in the young girl's form of address . . . .

There are no 'dead spirits' communicating through either mediums or channellers. There *are* demon spirits playing an impersonation game.

From Genesis to Revelation an anti-God force of great power and cunning is displayed in Scripture. He is arrogant and determined, the implacable foe of God and man, who is out to spoil and mar all that is good and lovely. He is there in the Garden of Eden at the beginning of the story. And he is there in the lake of fire at the Bible's end.

Dealing with fear. Is there any need to fear the Satanic supernatural?

Back about fifteen years ago, Doug Harris established The Reachout Trust. Its purpose? First, to help escapees from the world of cults and the occult. Second, to reach out to those deluded by cults and the occult with the message of the Gospel and the truth of the Bible.

Hence, as might be assumed, Doug Harris has just about as much experience as anyone in how to approach the murky realms of New Age and the occult. '*Are* they contacting the dead?' He was asked. He responded: 'No; they are contacting demons who are impersonating the dead.' He believes that the various doorways into the occult — astrology, ouija boards, psychic consultations, New Age books and films, TM, Yoga, Spiritualism, witchcraft and Satanism — lead to oppression or possession by evil spirits. By opening certain doors into their lives, individuals have given Satan permission to enter.

But, says Doug, 'Satan is no equal to the individual who has a relationship with the Living God. Because of God's supremacy, Satan's activities take place within certain clearly-defined parameters.' Satan is *not* free to use the terrors and tricks from his nightmare dimension — unless the individual opens a door to him and, by doing so, extends an invitation.

Deliverance. But what about those who, having allowed Satan into their lives, decide they want to be free of him?

Cherie, you will recall, banished Satan from her life and invited God's Holy Spirit in as a result of prayer and latching on to the Christian Gospel.

Doug Harris, for the benefit of those who want to reach out to those imprisoned by the occult, outlines four stages:

• *Deal with fear.* People should not seek to deal with a situation with an occult dimension unless they, themselves, have a close relationship with Jesus Christ and, through that relationship, have no fear of Satan. 'Fear', says Doug Harris, 'gives Satan a foothold. Be sure of your position in Christ.' '*Submit yourselves, then, to God. Resist the devil, and he will flee from you.*' James 4:7, emphasis supplied. There is much that the Old Testament, as well as the New, can teach us about deliverance.

The people of God were surrounded by 'a vast army' of God's enemies. The King of Israel was alarmed and fearful. Fear is a normal reaction for those coming into contact with the works of Satan for the first time. Perhaps previously they had given no credence to the supernatural or the paranormal. Fear at the outset is not wrong; but it is important what we do with that fear.

When the King was afraid he 'resolved to enquire of

the Lord'. All must seek God if they would help anyone in the thrall of occult forces. The King also told the people to seek God; similarly, those in the power of occult forces must want to be released.

The King reminded himself, 'Power and might are in your (God's) hand, and no one can withstand you.' The position of God is supremely powerful, a fact that must be acknowledged by all who would help in deliverance situations. First, having become aware of where the enemy is, we must lift up our eyes and behold the greatness of God.[1]

On another occasion in the Old Testament record, one of God's prophets, Elisha, was victimized by the King of Syria because he had informed the King of Israel of his intentions. Thus the enemy king sent 'horses and chariots and a strong force' to Dothan where Elisha lived. 'They went by night and surrounded the city.' At dawn Elisha's servant went out. Seeing that the city was surrounded by a powerful force, he panicked and, running in, blurted out to Elisha: 'Oh, my lord, what shall we do?'

Elisha's answer is very important; 'Don't be afraid. . . . Those who are with us are more than those who are with them.'

This was an outrageous proposition as far as Elisha's servant was concerned. All he could see were soldiers and horses and chariots surrounding the city. Then Elisha prayed, '"Oh Lord, open his eyes so that he may see."' Then the Lord opened the servant's eyes, and he looked and saw the hills full of horses and chariots of fire all around Elisha.[2]

Previously Elisha's servant had seen only what was in the natural realm. Elisha's prayer enabled him to see the supernatural forces — the armies of the invincible God — surrounding His prophet.

As we approach occult-related situations, it is imperative that, like Elisha's servant, we catch a vision of the unconquerable armies of the Almighty God. Yes, we must understand the schemes of Satan 'in order that Satan might not outwit us'.[3] But, first and foremost, we must acknowledge that God is supreme and that demons are powerless before Him.

• We must be aware of what the individual, caught up in the toils of the occult, is saying, and what he or she is not saying. 'Don't jump to the conclusion that you've got to cast out demons,' insists Doug Harris. 'Allow the Spirit of God to witness to you. Sometimes people need counselling in other areas . . . .' In Justin's case, for example, the situation was complex; there was a fine line between the physical and psychological consequences of drug abuse and Rave, and the evil voices.

• 'If it does become evident', says Doug Harris, 'that there is a demonic influence in the life, try to identify the doorway through which it has entered. This would involve questioning the individual in some detail. It may be necessary to rehearse the various doorways through which Satan gains access to a life; ouija boards, astrology, New Age crystals or channelling, contact with spiritualist practices, Rave, whatever. Once the doorway is identified, it must be shut, firmly.' How? 1. The individual must repent, must acknowledge that the occult practice was evil, and *must* be prepared to turn his or her back on it. 2. There must be prayer in the name of the Father, the Son and the Holy Spirit. In the name of the triune God the door must be pronounced closed and the demon banished. Thereafter, Satan has no right to that life any more. The sin has been confessed and, once confessed, sin is covered by the blood shed by Jesus on Calvary. After the demon has been banished in the name of Jesus, it has no longer any right to the life of that individual. The door has been shut.

• Doug Harris of The Reachout Trust is very emphatic about this one; 'Don't leave the life empty . . . .' The spirit of evil must be replaced by the Spirit of God. Prayer must be said that the Holy Spirit will enter and occupy the life of the individual released from the snares of Satan.

In the deliverance ministry experience of Doug Harris, it has rarely been the case that anything especially dramatic has happened at the point of deliverance. Sometimes, he says, there is 'a lifting of the atmosphere'; at other times a marked facial change, at still other times an evident change of character. 'Of vital importance,' says Doug, 'is that, having banished Satan and introduced the Holy Spirit, the individual must be affirmed, and built up in the Lord. God's Gospel of grace must be explained and he or she must be made aware that justification and new birth (an ongoing relationship with Jesus) is a daily experience.'

'Occult' and 'revelation'. By definition, *occult* is 'that which is hidden/concealed'. There are many places where the devil and his messages can be found; and Satan's most underestimated hide-out is Rock in its various forms.

The opposite of occult is *revelation*. Revelation means the act of exposing, taking the lid off something. And that is what Bible writers sought to do: to make us aware of the power of God and the transforming Gospel of Christ — *and* the stratagems of Satan.

The message of the Gospel? ''''You *must* be born again,'''' said Jesus.[4] Admit your need of God. Confess your sin-sorrow. Surrender your life to God. He is either Lord *of* all, or He is not Lord *at* all!

The Gospel of Jesus meets the deepest cries and needs

of men and women of all cultures, of all ages. He is the light in our darkness; the purpose in an otherwise purposeless life; the meaning in an otherwise meaningless existence.

We can enter a new life through a new birth. And it starts at the Cross.

Christ is the central figure in Scripture.

The Cross is its central symbol. All Scripture and (according to Scripture) all history lies beneath its shadow.

The very shape of the Cross suggests the length, breadth and height of the love of God. It points to heaven from where Jesus came. It is rooted in the earth He came to redeem. The outstretched hands on the transverse beam are an invitation to all men — even to His crucifiers.

Sin and guilt are left at the Cross. An old life can die there, and a new life be born. And that new life is the beginning of an everlasting adventure.

Every devil from wherever devils come from was present at Calvary. It was Satan's great chance to upset God's plan for the salvation of man.

But when Jesus died, there was a cry of triumph on His lips: 'It is finished!' 'Mission accomplished!'

Whooping for joy. The salvation of man was accomplished. Jesus had died as a sacrifice; died with the sins of the whole world upon His shoulders. Died for every man and woman who has lived and will ever live. By accepting Jesus as their Saviour, men and women can have forgiveness of sin and a new life. It happened to Cherie; and she is still whooping for joy!

New birth, above all, is why Calvary makes the devil tremble.

Calvary came right at the centre of the clash of the

two kingdoms; and it was (literally) the crux of the age-long conflict between good and evil. And in the clash of kingdoms, God's kingdom was victorious. The battle was won: by good and by God. Man was given freedom to choose *not* to be evil. And the devil's ultimate destruction was made certain.

Because of Calvary, Scripture can say, 'If we confess our sins, he is faithful and just and will forgive us our sins and purify us from all unrighteousness.'[5] '"If a man is thirsty, let him come to me and drink. Whoever believes in me, as the Scripture has said, streams of living water will flow from within him."'[6]

And Jesus made the unconditional promise that no one who comes to Him is ever turned away.[7]

But we have mentioned an end-time age and identified it with this one. We have expressed a paradox: that, in this end-time age, Satan is working frantically, knowing that his time is running out; but have we not said that the devil was defeated at Calvary?

How can we resolve the paradox?

And, given the devil's present-day hyperactivity, should not God's Book have given us some advanced warning?

---

[1] 2 Chronicles 20. [2] 2 Kings 6:12-18. [3] 2 Corinthians 2:11. [4] John 3:7, emphasis supplied. [5] 1 John 1:9. [6] John 7:37, 38. [7] John 6:37.

Note. David Burnett, *Unearthly Powers* (Marc, 1988), is an excellent introduction to the perception of the supernatural in different cultures.

Incoming Thunderheads

It has. And in some detail.

Three times in the last chapter of the Bible, Jesus promises: 'Yes, I am coming soon.'[1] That promise has echoed down the arches of the ages and is the hope of Christians today.

The words were spoken by Jesus, but written by John. Nineteen hundred years ago John, branded as a dangerous criminal, was banished to the rocky island of Patmos. He had been one of the close associates of Jesus, and his treachery was in his persistent assertion that the Christ the Romans had crucified had risen to life — and would return to earth in power and glory. Such ideas were considered a threat to the political stability of the Roman Empire.

On his lonely Mediterranean rock, John received visions of a final holocaust. He wrote them down and sent them to his revolutionary brothers on the mainland. They were secretly copied, circulated, and compiled into a book that later became known as the Apocalypse or the Revelation. Although written in a time of bows and spears, these visions teach ideas that make sense only when placed in the context of the developments of our modern age and of our modern technology.

The return. John's Apocalypse, with the complementary book of Daniel in the Old Testament, contains a time-scheme. From Daniel's time-schedule, wise men had calculated, accurately, the date of Christ's first coming. From the time-prognoses of Daniel and the Revelation, however, it is *not* possible to calculate the actual time of Christ's second coming. Not surprising, that. Jesus

Himself had been emphatic that the timing of His coming was God's secret.[2]

On average, the Second Coming is referred to once in every twenty-five verses of the New Testament.

On oath and on trial for his life, Jesus told the Jewish Ruling Council, '"I say to all of you: In future you will see the Son of Man sitting at the right hand of the Mighty One and coming on the clouds of heaven."'[3]

While references to the Coming, and to the signs that will precede it, are scattered throughout the New Testament, Jesus had far more to say about both His coming and the signs than anyone else had.[4]

Counterfeits. In His list of signs-to-look-out-for, Jesus placed the appearance of 'false christs and false prophets'. In a decade in which both thought-leaders and Rock stars are, in the words of John White, prophesying that 'channelling will soon be considered the norm rather than the exception', everyone with his own 'spirit guide',[5] it's time to pause for thought. New Age has provided a plethora of false prophets and channelled any number of false christs, not to mention the Lord Maitreya who they say is waiting in the wings, a new world messiah to preside over a new world order.

So called 'New Age Christians' preach that Christ will appear separately in inner rooms and desert locations — *exactly* as Jesus said they would. His advice? 'If anyone tells you, "There he is, out in the desert" do not go out; or, "Here he is, in the inner rooms," do not believe it.' Satan's ability to counterfeit is limited. And the real Second Advent will be the most audible and visual event since the creation of the world; 'For as the lightning comes from the east and flashes to the west, so will be the coming of the Son of man.'[6]

At this moment both Rock and Rave — 'the birth canals', you may remember, 'of the New Age' — pose major threats to the minds of a whole generation, and New Age itself is vaunted as a viable alternative to Christianity. All the false prophets of New Age, and those who have used their skills to saturate contemporary media output and pop culture with New Age ideas and outright Satanism, together with the fat cats who have profited from the drug culture that has ruined the lives of millions, and the pagan Rock-Rave culture that has blown the minds of tens of thousands, will, at last, face God's anger.[7]

Jesus reserved His sternest warnings, firstly, for those who set out to lead youth into sin;[8] and, secondly, for those who pervert the Gospel of Christ and substitute bad religion.[9] Because of the Greek root of the word translated 'false christs', it is thought likely that Jesus was also warning against 'false anointings'; non-biblical manifestations in the Christian Church attributed — blasphemously — to the Holy Spirit.

Storms at midnight. 'We do not want you to be ignorant about those who fall asleep,' wrote Paul the apostle, 'or to grieve like the rest of men, who have no hope . . . .'[10] And Paul goes on to provide, arguably, the most graphic description of all of the Second Coming of Jesus Christ, when those who have died in Christ will respond to the trumpet call of God and rise to meet Jesus returning through skies full-brilliant with angels. But before that great day can come, warns Paul, there will be a major crisis in the Church, in society, and in world affairs. It will be centred around a movement that will exalt its leader who, in turn, will 'exalt himself over everything that is called God or is worshipped . . . , proclaiming himself to be God'. That movement and its leader will co-operate with Satanic displays and occult 'counterfeit miracles, signs and wonders', that will deceive a great many. 'A powerful delusion' will fog the minds of the people and distort their thinking.[11]

In the Apocalypse, writing from Patmos, John described a coalition of forces that would provide Satan with a hands-on role in world affairs in the generation immediately before the coming of Jesus. This false trinity of powers would employ the 'spirits of demons' and occult miracles.[12]

'In conclusion be strong — not in yourselves but in the Lord, in the power of his boundless resource,' wrote the apostle Paul. 'Put on God's complete armour so that you can successfully resist all the devil's methods of attack. For our fight is not against any physical enemy: it is against organizations and powers that are spiritual. We are up against the unseen power that controls this dark world, and spiritual agents *from the very headquarters of evil* . . . .'[13]

There *is* a conspiracy; but it is not a conspiracy of Hollywood honchos and moguls, Rock's headliners and hellcats, nor the gurus of false religion. The conspiracy is far more dangerous; it involves a hierarchy of bloodless entities 'from the very headquarters of evil' — with Satan at the top.

Spiritualism, with its seances, mediums, voices and ectoplasm was just a beginning.

New Age — with its channellers, and crystals, and gurus, and masters, and deep-throated voices claiming to speak the wisdom of the ages but, in fact, articulating the deceptions of the Satanic realm — is a more major threat to the cause of Christ.

Why?

• Because New Age covers so much ground and some of it is good ground. It has so many faces, and many of them are pleasant faces.

- Its first approach to the world is an appealing one and, because part of that appeal is insinuated into Rock lyrics, it is absorbed by minds rendered vacuous and susceptible by Techno Pagan and Rave.

- Because it has so much influence in the movies and the media.

- Because it has made so many doors and created a climate in which members of the younger generation, in particular, are disposed to open those doors and allow influences from the very headquarters of evil into their minds and lives.

- And because it has such a major influence on our educational system. Jenny Hinton, the daughter of the New Age priestess who founded Findhorn, but who abandoned her mother's brand of paganism for the cause of Christ, has spent many years researching the evidence of those influences and has presented them in an impressive analysis. For many US Christians, New Age influence in the classroom is their primary concern.[14]

- Because Yoga and New Age meditation techniques are employed by all major companies to control stress and enhance salesmanship and management expertise. These companies include all the major multi nationals. *Fortune* magazine reports that half of America's 500 top businesses are engaged in New Age 'human potential training' (accepted by Christians as the entering wedge to the occult).[15]

- Finally, because the Christian Churches are doing so little, firstly, to warn of the perils of New Age and the avenues through which it works; and, secondly, to present the Christian Gospel in the language and thought-forms of the younger generation.

In particular, at times it appears that the Church

responds with little more than embarrassed silence to the counter culture's allegation that God must accept responsibility for all the world's suffering . . . .

[1]Revelation 22:7, 12, 20. [2]Matthew 24:36. [3]Matthew 26:64. [4]Matthew 24; Mark 13; Luke 17:22-36; 21:5-36; John 14:1-3. [5]John White, 'Channelling, a Short History of a Long Tradition', *Holistic Life Magazine* (Summer 1985), page 22; *The Sunday Review* in *The Independent on Sunday*, 5 January 1997. [6]Matthew 24:26, 27. [7]Revelation 20:9, 10. [8]Luke 17:1, 2. [9]Galatians 1:6-9; Matthew 23. [10]1 Thessalonians 4:13-18. [11]2 Thessalonians 2:1-12; 2 Timothy 3:1-7; 2 Peter 2:1-12; 3:3-14; Jude 3-8. [12]Revelation 16:12-16. See Revelation 12:3, 4, 7-9; chapter 13:13. [13]Ephesians 6:10-12, Phillips, emphasis supplied. [14]Jenny Hinton, *Influence of New Age in British Education* (self published, June 1992); Russell Chandler, *Understanding the New Age* (Word, 1989), pages 153-157. See Neil Anderson, *The Seduction of our Children* (Harvest House, 1991), pages 62, 63. [15]Walter Martin, *The New Age Cult* (Bethany House Publishers, 1989), pages 61, 64, 71, 72; *God's of the New Age*, video (Riverside Films, 1984); *Time*, 7 December 1987; Patricia King and Penelope Wang, 'The Karma of Capitalism', *Newsweek*, 3 August 1987; Jeremy Main, 'Trying to Bend Managers' Minds', *Fortune Magazine*, 23 November 1987.

Good God. Bad World. Why?

'Some might say they don't believe in heaven;
Go and tell it to the man who lives in hell.'
— Oasis, 'Some Might Say' (1996)

Oasis lead singer, Liam Gallagher, frequently signs into hotels as 'Lucifer' and has told the tabloids: 'I want to go to hell because the devil has all the good times.'[1]

This kind of 'in-your-face, God!' was a theme running through many pop lyrics during 1996. Everyone from Manic Street Preachers, through Blur and Bon Jovi to Michael Jackson and George Michael were on to it.

The lyric writers, apparently, are abreast of the fact that not all is right with the world — and they want to hold God responsible.

They're not on their own. One of the top people's papers ran a 'profile on God' following a particularly gruesome massacre. The writer held God responsible for every war, famine and atrocity from the beginning of recorded time to late last night. Then, in one final 'In-your-face!' sentence he managed to imply that God didn't actually exist! You might say he had it both ways![2]

The tendency to blame God for all the evil that surrounds us is nothing new. At one time or another, all the great Christians have done it! Martin Luther said that, for all of us, there are days when faith trembles on the brink and we ask, 'Where is God? Can it be true?'

'MUMMY, DON'T BLAME JESUS. IT'S NOT HIS FAULT' was the banner headline in my local newspaper a couple of years ago. Those were, apparently, the dying words of 8-year-old Andrew Pickering, losing a fourteen-month battle with leukaemia. But Andrew's reaction was untypical. It was so unusual, in fact, that a religious musical has been written around it and performed to vast audiences.

When disaster strikes, some come right out and blame God. Others, bemused, cry, 'Why?' Still others ask, in bewilderment, 'Where have you gone, God?' Michelle, and, to some extent, Justin, asked this question, following the death of their mother. Finding no immediate answer, Michelle responded with anger.

God is love. But what about agony, evil, confusion, heartache and pain? The world is often dark and the heavens are always silent. How *can* God be love?

The Why? question is as old as sin because pain is the same age, and premature death, almost as old.

The Bible does not shy away from the 'Good God. Bad world. Why?' question.

The book of Job affirms that bad things *do* happen to good people, that God is *not* a sort of cosmic vending machine ensuring that good behaviour buys pleasure, bad behaviour buys pain. Job, probably the oldest book in Scripture, was written to counter this notion. It lays down the parameters within which we can pursue the 'Why?' question, and it keeps us from losing our way.

The first principle: *God is in control.* Everything that happens has to be sieved through His sovereign power, and limitless love and grace. Everything that happens can be made to serve some purpose. We are not merely victims of chaos.

The second principle: the book of Job makes it clear that *God is not the author of evil.*

The third principle: *God's presence is the only real solution to suffering.* Job, like Isaiah, heard God's assurance: 'When you pass through the waters, I will be with you; and when you pass through the rivers, they will not sweep over you. When you walk through the fire, you will not be burned; the flames will not set you ablaze. For I am the Lord . . . your Saviour.'[3]

Though there are times when there are more questions than answers, there are at least a few things that the Christian Church has learned after twenty centuries of agonizing with the problem of suffering:

- **If you believe that God is a God of love, you have the problem of evil. But if you do not believe that God is a God of love, you have a million problems.**

For every thousand people who vocalize the question, 'Why is there evil?' there is no one to raise the far bigger question, 'Why is there good?'

When BBC News reader Martyn Lewis asked if it would be possible for the News team to feature one item of *good* news each day, fellow News reader Peter Sissons replied that to report good news would not be to report reality.

What did Sissons mean by reality? He meant variations from the norm; the calamities that grab the headlines. Virtue, fulfilled lives, healthy people, loving families and incident-free travel do not make news. Yet they are the norm of life. The norm of life is good: daily food, the ordinary use of our faculties, the unhindered enjoyment of our lives. But because they *are* the norm they are unremarkable and, therefore, not newsworthy.

But if there is no God of love, how do we explain that all our faculties do not minister pain to us? That the norm of life *is* good? That there are noble, altruistic motives, high-minded, love-driven ambitions, great causes, selflessness?

• God is a God of law. He made a universe, not a multiverse.

The universe is based on the rule of law. All worthwhile things depend upon the reliability of natural law. Without it there would be no agriculture, no science, no life. Though God, from time to time, sets aside His own laws to perform a miracle, if He did it all the time the universe would become anarchic. Further, if He did it only for those who love Him, His adversary in the Clash of Kingdoms would be able to say that people served Him from wrong motives.

• God gave man freedom of choice. He created man as a free agent, not a robot. But by giving man freedom God, in effect, placed limitations on His own freedom of action. (Soren Kierkegaard.)

We choose, act on our own choices — and are left to experience the consequences. It's an aspect of freedom. Heart disease and cancer are responsible for 74 per cent of all deaths — and medical opinion is united in the view that, in the great majority of cases, these diseases are preventable. Life-style is the major determining factor in health and longevity. Many in our society commit suicide — by knife and fork. C. S. Lewis estimated that four fifths of human suffering is man-made.

It is worth remembering that man, not God, invented bows, bullets, bayonets, bombs and inter-continental ballistic missiles . . . .

During one period of sacred history, God *did* get involved in a more direct way in the detailed lives of His people. It was the period between the Exodus and the point when the Israelites reached the frontiers of the Promised Land. But the generation that witnessed some of God's most remarkable interventions on behalf of His people — the parting of the Red Sea, the daily miracle of manna and the thunder from Sinai — lived in fear of God. And fear produced rebellion. For most of the Old Testament, God depended upon word of mouth — through His prophets. People could choose to listen or not to listen.

Then God *really* became involved. The sovereign God imprisoned Himself in human flesh and came to live as a member of a poor family, in a town with a bad name on the planet He wanted to save. He came personally to encounter and to conquer suffering and pain and sin and death. He came to save man from the consequences of his own bad choices . . . .

• **Is it possible — in some cases — that pain and suffering have a purpose?**

C. S. Lewis, in *The Problem of Pain*, called pain 'God's megaphone', God's means of attracting our attention when all His other means have been exhausted. Is it possible that God *does* permit pain or distress — *in some cases* — in order to attract our attention?

When Lewis married Joy Gresham, he was placed in a situation in which he had to rethink his position on pain. Within three or four years, he was obliged to watch her dying of cancer.[4] Afterwards, he wrote another book and published it anonymously: *A Grief Observed*. He described the bleak experience in which, even when he cried out to God, it seemed to him that a door was slammed in his face and that he heard the sounds of bolting and double bolting on the other side. It was months before he realized that God was on the same side of the door as he was. And, as with Job, he discovered that the real healing for the pain of bereavement was found in the presence of God and in the comfort God provides.

Depending upon our attitude, we can be made either bitter or better by life's hard knocks.

John Donne (1571-1631) wrote, 'I need thy thunder, Oh my God; Thy music will not serve Thee . . . .' After a number of failed career ventures, Donne found fulfilment in the Gospel ministry. But, only weeks into his new career, his wife died, leaving him with seven children. . . . Nevertheless, he soldiered on to become Dean of St Paul's Cathedral and the most popular preacher of his time. It was at that time that he displayed the symptoms of the Bubonic Plague. Was it time to give up on God? Donne thought not. Looking death in the face day by day and hour by hour, he wrote his *Devotions*, the most incisive manuscript ever written about suffering. He expressed a faith in the God who, beyond the death of death, would make all things new, make all things plain, and provide answers to all his questions. 'One short sleep past/We wake eternally/And death shall be no more/ Death, thou shalt die.'

Donne survived to preach another day. He believed God had been shouting to attract his attention when he had failed to hear the heavenly music . . . .

Our mental attitude and whether we are prepared to lean on God may determine whether our adversities will make us bitter or better . . . .

• God, the Sufferer.

Great Christians, like Jennifer Rees Larcombe, after long years of suffering, have testified to the experience of the close presence of God and to the belief that God suffers when we suffer, and then some.[5]

But many, in their adversity and suffering, feel let down by man and by God. There was a time when Jesus knew what it was to feel forsaken by man and to feel that God was a measureless gulf away. On Calvary He cried out: 'My God, My God, why . . . .' But through this death — the ultimate involvement — it was made possible for men and women of every age to choose Christ as their Champion and find pardon, peace, joy and eternity. The resurrection of Jesus meant the conquest of death. The ascension of Jesus made possible the coming of the Comforter. And the Comforter, the Holy Spirit, provides the close presence of God as we face the worst of life's adversities.

But Calvary was D-Day. V-Day is still to come. Calvary made it certain that sin, Satan and death would be destroyed. But the alien force exposed in Job would continue to do its worst — until V-Day. And it is doing its worst right now.

On V-Day Jesus returns in glory. Then all wrongs will be righted. Then, person to person, we shall meet Him and have our questions answered. Meanwhile, like Andrew Pickering, we must hold on to faith; 'Mummy, don't blame Jesus — it's not His fault.' Jesus said, '"You do not realize now what I am doing, but later you will understand."'[6]

When suffering strikes we can choose between the Jacob response and the Joseph response. The Jacob response? 'All these things are against me.' The Joseph response? 'Man meant this for evil, but God meant it for good.' God is an expert at bringing the best out of the worst possible situations.

Pain and suffering are inevitable. Misery is optional.

[1]Vivienne James. *Daily Mirror*, February 1996. [2]*The Independent on Sunday*, 3 March 1996. [3]Isaiah 43:2, 3. [4]Brian Sibley, *Shadowlands* (HarperCollins, 1991). [5]David Marshall, *Is God Still in the Healing Business?* (Autumn House, 1994). [6]See John 13:7.

The Monster's Riddle

According to legend, a monster lived outside the city of Thebes. It must have been a talking monster, because it posed a riddle to all wanting to get in or out of the city. If they couldn't answer the riddle, the monster destroyed them. The riddle: 'What has two legs, three legs, four legs; and is weakest when it has most legs?' People were slain every day because they couldn't answer the riddle. Then Oedipus, the son of the King, answered it: 'The answer to the riddle is man. Man has two legs; but as an infant he's on all fours — that's when he's weakest; then, when he's old, he uses a stick — he's on three legs.' And so Oedipus saved the city.

The world sets each of us a riddle. On finding an answer to that riddle depends joy, peace, a sense of purpose in this life — and eternity. Man is not the answer to this riddle. Man *is* the riddle.

There are questions we all must answer: 'Who am I?' 'What am I doing here?' 'Where am I going?' 'What is the purpose of life?' 'Is it just a dusty shuffle across a desert from Point Birth to Point Death — or is there some grand universal purpose?' Unless we answer those questions, life is empty, aimless and meaningless. Our relationships with others break down. We walk around with a civil war inside us. And, at last, the universe destroys us, and we fade into eternal oblivion.

The most urgent problem you have to face is the one in your mirror. On the solution you arrive at, depends what you think you are, and how important your decisions are. If life is 'a tale told by an idiot, full of sound and fury signifying nothing', then, what does anything matter? Lust, hate, murder, rape, lying, stealing — so what!

A bubble or an egg? But what if life *does* have meaning? What if there *is* something supremely worth doing? Supremely worth being? There are two alternatives. Life has to be a bubble or an egg. Which? If it's a bubble, it will end in a sticky mess. If it's an egg, it will end in a new life.

In their song titled 'A Design', released in 1996, the group Manic Street Preachers included these two lines:

> *We don't talk about love,*
> *We only want to get drunk.*

And, before we die laughing at their stupidity, let's admit that many people answer the question 'What is life for?' along similar lines. Whether they put it into words or not, the answer that a lot of people seem to arrive at boils down to: 'Give me pleasure.' Unless you really tackle the Monster's riddle, the riddle of life, you end up thinking of existence as a meaningless meander through chaos, from accidental birth to insignificant death, and resolve to occupy the time grabbing and grasping material things and pursuing pleasure. 'Life exists for pleasure,' said Kurt Cobain, not long before his suicide. 'We're here for kicks.' But 'life is for pleasure' is a worn-out swindle. Even the most intense pleasures are short-lived. The trouble is you don't know that the life-is-for-pleasure theorem is a swindle — until you've been swindled. For every 'kick' there's a kick back.

The pursuit-of-pleasure motif trumpeted by the Rock industry helps to account for the incidence of suicide among those involved in it. The almost universal pursuit of pleasure accounts for the fact that suicide is one of the main causes of death in the Western world. It's more common among Whites than Blacks, haves than have-nots. People have plumped for 'Pleasure' as the answer to the Monster's Riddle, and have found it to be an answer answerless.

The monsters. There are certain monsters that stalk all of us. It doesn't matter if I'm a president, prime minister, company director — or Dougal the dustman. The monsters are the same: sin, sorrow, guilt, death and judgement.

But life has a simplicity about it: Solve the sin problem and you have all the rest licked. Start by tackling any of the other problems and you won't get anything licked. Because death and judgement are still at the end.

Everyone must solve the Monster's Riddle. Everyone must find a solution to the sin problem.

People can laugh at the story of Genesis 1-3, but they can't laugh the results of it out of their bones, out of their body chemistry, out of their heads, out of their homes, out of the hells on earth they make for themselves.

The Internet has just thrown this up on the screen. Between 1500 BC and the last news bulletin, there have been circa 3,000 wars in the Western world. Apparently, civilized man has spent most of his time waging war. This is a symptom of his sickness. Man *is* sick. That's the message of modern literature, modern art and, above all, the modern music we have analysed in this book.

Man is sick. And the sickness is the sickness of sin. Sin is the reality that breaks hearts, blights homes, and robs heaven. There's no one without it. No one at all. Solving the sin problem is the most fundamental issue of life.

Solving the Monster's Riddle involves solving the sin problem. Sin is a deadly cancer that eats at the souls of men. Because of sin, every news cast is darkened by horror and atrocity. Because of sin, every road through life is hazardous, every voyage perilous. It destroys happiness, warps personalities, darkens the understanding, leads to under-achievement, sears the conscience. Sin is responsible for all sorrow, all pain, all misery. Sin has a scintillating, even psychedelic exterior; but on the inside there is sorrow, pain, misery — and millions of ruined lives. It promises liberty — it gives addiction; it promises champagne — it gives vinegar; it promises silk — it gives sacking. Sin is the most deceptive thing in the universe — and it dwells in you and in me.

The riddle we have to solve. The Monster's Riddle is the sin problem. Solving the sin problem is basic for time and eternity. For time, solving the sin problem means purpose, peace, and fulfilment. Solving the sin problem for eternity — well, unless you solve the sin problem there will be no eternity; solve it — and eternity is a reality beyond your most adventurous imaginings.

Scripture says that sin is a disease that will prove terminal unless cured by a radical method. Searching for a cure does not mean dwelling on the disease, however; concentrate on your sins and you become more sinful. Nevertheless, finding that cure must be life's first priority.

If you make it your first priority, Jesus said, God will look after everything else in your life.[1]

'Forgetting what is behind,' said Paul, 'I press on towards the goal to win the prize.'[2]

Of Mary it was said, 'She's got it right. She sits at the feet of Jesus, looking to Him for the answer. She has found it.'[3]

Lots of people feel no need to find a solution to the Monster's Riddle. Many profess self-sufficiency. Then the crisis comes and they crack up. Most people have the clearest view of life's priorities when they are in a crisis.

There is an urgency about solving that riddle. But in your pursuit of a solution to the sin problem, the first thing you have to learn is that there is no do-it-yourself method.

And now the Good News. . . . The monsters that stalk you have been felled, beaten, destroyed: sin, sorrow, death and the rest. There's One who came as your Champion who did what you could not do for yourself. Your sins were nailed to His cross. *He* is your answer to the sin problem.

Through the death of His Son, God reconciled us to Himself. And, if we repent and ask, we may receive the solution to the sin problem as a gift: salvation through the Christ of Calvary.[4]

The price for your sin has been paid. It was paid 2,000 years ago by your Saviour Substitute, Jesus Christ. If, that is, you accept Him as your Saviour.

The devil may still be frantically active — working like mad to recruit subjects for his infernal kingdom — but he's a beaten enemy. When Christ was lifted up on the Cross, the kingdom of hell crumbled. It was D-Day for the devil, and he knew it.[5]

By His death, Jesus destroyed 'him who holds the power of death — that is, the devil'.[6]

Jesus, perfect, righteous — the only Man who has ever loved good infinitely and hated evil infinitely. Why did He die? Because our sins were credited to Him: our skeletons in the cupboard, the things we did in the darkness — or in the open. The strange transaction at the heart of the Good News is that when we accept Him as our Saviour, in return for our sin, He gives us His goodness. His goodness makes possible our salvation.[7]

That strange transaction — the Good News about Jesus — is the solution to life's riddle, the Monster's

Riddle, that all must solve to live life to the full here, and to enjoy eternity.

God gave us life and health and talents. God invented sex and beauty and everything that's enjoyable. And what do we give Him? Our sins, our ingratitude, our impurity, our malice, our selfishness. Jesus bore all this to the Cross, died for it — and recalls us to new, fulfilled, high-level living.

Accept no substitute! That's the real thing!

• At best, Rock-Rave is an anaesthetic. At worst, it blows your brain and sinks you down to lower than animal level.

• At best, drugs mess you up. At worst, they kill you. Sometimes instantly, sometimes slowly.

• And the occult, the third factor implicated in Justin's suicide, is the terrain of terror for dupes bent on destruction. An invitation — signed, sealed, delivered — to an alien force. An alien force all too willing to enter your life, to take away your freedom, your big break, and your little breaks too — until life is inside out, upside down, schizoid and terrifying, no longer worth living.

Who would take that, when high-level living is on offer?

The enemies of Jesus said, 'This man receives sinners,' and meant it to sting. But they spoke true. And the truth they spoke is your hope of a happy life, and the deep joy of being sure of eternity.

'All kinds of sin and blasphemy shall be forgiven to those who repent,' said Jesus. So there is hope, regardless of your past. Jesus claimed the power to erase your past with pardon.

'No one who comes to me', said Jesus, 'will ever be turned away . . . .'[8]

Jesus has overcome our enemies: the world, the flesh, and the devil.

He has killed all the monsters that stalk us and, in Christ, the devil's nightmare dimension need hold no terrors for us.

Keep the doors tight shut where the devil might enter. If you are 'in Christ' there is nothing to fear. Not the Satanic world beloved of the Rock lyric writers. Not the demons conjured up by the mediums and the channellers. No demon, not even the arch-demon, is a match for the individual with Christ on his side.[9]

We've had the iron age, the age of steam, and the space age. And now we find ourselves in the age of grot. It's on the magazine racks. It's on at the cinema. There's grot on cassette, grot on CD, grot on TV at random — and grot on the Internet. And behind the grot is a grot business, and fat cats getting rich from it. They employ the image-beamers who, by every audio-visual refinement of technology, aim to monopolize your five senses with what is, at best, chewing gum for the mind and, at worst, slow-acting poison.

Whatever gets your attention, gets you.

On our own, we're feeble in the face of the image-beamers. In Christ, we're invincible.

The Monster's Riddle has been solved. The sin problem is solved by coming to the Saviour. And, as far as He is concerned, it's a come-as-you-are party. If you wait until you're 'good enough', you'll wait for ever. He welcomes the guttermost as well as the uttermost. And the place where we must meet Him is at the foot of the Cross.

Remember, whatever gets your attention, gets you . . . .

---

[1]See Matthew 6:33. [2]Philippians 3:13, 14. [3]See Luke 10:38-42. [4]Romans 5:1, 2, 6, 8-11. [5]John 12:31, 32. [6]Hebrews 2:14. [7]2 Corinthians 5:21. [8]See John 6:37. [9]Romans 6.